Do Not Go Gentle.
Go to Paris.

To Fran —
we strong ladies need
to stick together! Onward!

Gail Schelling

Do Not Go Gentle.
Go to Paris.

Travels of an Uncertain Woman
Of a Certain Age

Gail Thorell Schilling

ISBN-13: 978-1-0956-5380-7

Library of Congress Control Number: 2019909427

Grateful acknowledgement is made to the following for permission to reprint previously published material: "Do Not Go Gentle Into That Good Night" By Dylan Thomas, from THE POEMS OF DYLAN THOMAS, copyright ©1952 by Dylan Thomas. Reprinted by permission of New Directions Publishing Corporation, United States of America. Reprinted by permission of The Dylan Thomas Trust, United Kingdom.

The author met many people during her travels. Some names and identifying details have been changed to protect their privacy.

Published by Kindle Direct Publishing, Seattle, WA.

Book cover design by Bespoke Book Covers.

Dedication

For my children Tess, Greg, Tom, and Trina
who made me brave.

Table of Contents

Preface

In 2010, thanks to an extraordinary confluence of events, I flew out of my life and into the daydream I'd been safeguarding for 40 years: travel to Paris and a solo month in France. I smile now as I remember how "old" I felt at 62 – almost 10 years ago.

Back then, I had no access to emerging technology such as GPS, iPhone (phone, camera, or mobile Internet). Instead, I managed email at the few scattered Internet cafes; used a phone card with public phones, flummoxed by rapid-fire French instructions; and lugged a separate digital camera, small laptop, and bulky voltage converter. As an independent traveler, I had to find my way by trusting my wits. I had to depend upon the kindness of strangers and divine grace. Perhaps they are the same.

I'm convinced that depending on electronic devices would have lessened my learning curve and the spritz of exhilaration I felt each time I solved a problem, however modest. Instead, self-reliance evolved into the self-trust that came to define my journey. I arranged my own itinerary and booked my own lodging online without help from a travel agent; I had not yet learned about Airbnb, a fledgling service. Online booking was still evolving and precarious, warned travel sites. Would the actual lodging match the online photos? Creepy stories abounded. Less-progressive hotels required credit card information via email: "Send half your credit card number in one email and half in another." Pure intuition steered me away from posting my credit card number in any way on the Internet.

Of course, much of this communication was in French years before I learned the joys of Google Translate and other language apps. Instead, I had to refresh my mothballed French skills. That I had read Camus's *Le Mythe de Sisyphe* (The Myth of Sisyphus) and Sartre's *Huis Clos* (No Exit) in French during university years didn't help much now. What did help was sharing pizza at the French table at the community college where I taught. Here, beginning students and I conversed, and I was pleased how much French I remembered. The French professor praised my accent. Practice buoyed my confidence. I just needed to relax and *talk*. Both at home and abroad, I discovered that conversation depends upon effort and goodwill much more than flawless grammar. I laughed at my many *faux pas* – and learned better French because of them. By the time I reached France, I could approach strangers with aplomb. Except for two harried clerks at train stations, I was always treated with the very same courtesy with which I approached others, even in Paris.

Along my journey, I found myself drawn to sacred spaces, usually very old churches. Perhaps I found these massive stone buildings to be, not simply beautiful, but safe places, quite literally sanctuaries, in cities where no one knew my name. Perhaps I subconsciously identified with the aged architecture: venerable, enduring … and an anachronism in a rat race world. During this time, sex abuse scandals erupted like boils within the Roman Catholic Church. Perhaps I sought to reassure myself that an exquisitely beautiful cathedral could transcend such moral depravity, that the work of human hands could atone for human offenses.

About a year after my trip to France, I received a fellowship at the Jentel Artist Community to write this memoir. To afford more time to write, I made my next bold decision: give up my apartment and find rent-free shelter as a house sitter, dog sitter, cat sitter, even chicken sitter. When I ran out of sitting gigs, friends and family offered lodging for weeks at a time. In this way, I could subsist on part-time work. My belongings lived in my daughter's basement -- until her flood. Whatever survived spent another two years in a storage locker. Four years after I flew to Paris, I finally settled into my own apartment, my nest. My age no longer bothers me. After all, it's the cornerstone of wisdom.

I hope that this book will inspire women, especially those of a certain age, to trust themselves. There is still time.

Concord, New Hampshire
March 2019

Chapter 1
Do Not Go Gentle. Go to Paris.

Do not go gentle into that good night,
Old age should burn and rage at close of day ...
– Dylan Thomas

Tricky knees. Silvery roots. Wrinkles and age spots. Unreliable bladder. Worse memory. Retirement only a few coins in the sugar bowl. And now, just before Christmas, the rules change mid-game: my writing courses go to a youngster with a better degree – but not my experience. My self-confidence sags like the skin under my arms. Without a professional identity, who am I? Without my four children at home, who needs me? Mon Cher cautiously courts me from 600 miles away. If we ever make it to romance, will I find my warranty expired? Menopause hijacked my estrogen long ago. Am I even a real woman anymore? So how am I supposed to grow old? Do I have to? I don't want to, no, not at all.

My son Tom, the globetrotter, is incensed by my being riffed at work. He responds with a handmade Christmas card, which is a map of France entwined in Christmas lights and Italy wearing a Santa hat. "Mumsy, it's time to set a date." With reckless generosity, Tom, a frugal grad student, gives me airfare to Europe, the journey I've deferred for 40 years. "Pick your dates, Mom! I'm booking it tonight." If Ed McMahon and the Publishers' Clearing House van had arrived on my doorstep, I couldn't have been more flabbergasted.

I eagerly plunge into this madcap plan and decide that I will explore only France and leave Italy for another time. But when? I consider the merits of leaving immediately, but I'd forfeit my few lower-level courses. I settle on dates in May when the weather will be warm and final exams will be over. Rashly, I decide to travel for an entire month to make up for lost decades, rationalizing that I have earned a day for each year I postponed my trip. Thanks to my most delirious senior moment ever, I overlook the inconvenient fact that not only will I need funds to bankroll the trip, I'll generate no income while I'm away.

When the Iceland Air confirmation pops up in my email, I know that this is real. Dear Lord! I need a place to stay! Here it is January, and I'm leaving in May! I hastily book a hostel bunk in Reykjavik, Iceland, my stopover; a piddling $3.80 holds my reservation. Tom magically secures his literature professor's home in Languedoc, France, for a couple of nights' free lodging. Only 27 more reservations to go and they need to be cheap-cheap; for aside from my reduced, break-even salary this semester, I have no extra money. So, where's the woman I used to be, the one who could squeeze the "get" out of budget?

Years ago in Wyoming, when my husband left me with four children, ages 2, 4, 5, and 8, I learned that all things are possible; the impossible just takes a little longer. The kiddos and I lived on hope and antelope, on faith and veggies gleaned from friends' gigantic gardens. I tracked down gently used clothes. I worked oddball jobs like goat wrangler, freelance writer, camp cook, and funeral soloist. I even skinned and butchered moose and elk provided by the Game and Fish folks. For 18 months, I reluctantly accepted Food Stamps when the child support dried up, but embarrassed beyond words, drove 12 miles to the next town to use them.

A "broken family?" Not at all. Sure, my erstwhile spouse had disappeared, but from a life of loose ends and raveled dreams, my kiddos, community, and I wove the fabric of family and earned the respect and generosity of our small mountain town. Providing for my children despite deprivation made me strong back then. Now I wonder, am I still strong or do we lose resiliency and resourcefulness when they're no longer actively needed? By being brave, even once, do we inoculate our souls against future crises of confidence? Perhaps like the flu, we'll just have a milder case.

Despite my tattered budget, a 60% pay cut, a payment plan with the IRS, bargain basement health insurance, and unpredictable employment, I rally faith and determination forged during 25 years in Big Sky. There I learned the rodeo mantra: "Let 'er buck and hang on for the buzzer!" I must ransom my dream, not just to see Europe, but to reassure myself that I can navigate my elder years independently, confidently. I have nothing left to lose except my self-respect. No, I will "not go gentle." I will go to Paris.

I had meant to go to Europe when I was 23, but like the besotted maiden in the ballad who gave her love a cherry that had no stone, I, too, did the impossible: I gave my love my life savings, so he could buy a boat -- even though he didn't know how to sail. We married. When that boat wasn't big enough, he bought another and within a month sank it. We made the first payment when it lay under 60 feet of Atlantic Ocean. Boat repairs, a mortgage, and children quickly followed. Whenever I'd suggest my long-postponed trip to Europe, perhaps for our tenth or 15th anniversary, he'd counter, "What do you have left after an expensive trip? Just a bunch of pictures." After 16 years of thwarting each other's dreams, we went our separate ways.

Paris, beautiful and romantic, had floated like a mirage on the edge of my consciousness for years. As my 60th birthday approached, my friend Marci and I vaguely planned to visit The City of Lights. But my San Francisco friend clearly enjoyed luxury; I preferred modest accommodations. She loved to shop and talk; I preferred window shopping and writing. Our plans fell by the wayside, but other friends bought into my romantic notions and sent me guidebooks and calendars of Paris. "We move toward that which we think about," said my professor in ED 140, Achieving Your Potential, the class that 20 years earlier had helped me to teach myself to be positive. I had tacked a small photo of the Eiffel Tower on my bulletin board at work. *I will think about Paris – and I will keep moving toward it.* Like the "impossible" challenges raising my kiddos, my "impossible" route to Paris just took longer, that's all.

During a February funk in 2008, I read that come summer, Québec City would celebrate its 400th birthday. Suddenly 60 didn't seem so old anymore. Much of the travel literature described Québec City as "North American Paris." Smaller, yes, and cheaper, but still beautifully French. Carol, my friend since college who loved roughing it and who would rather tear out a wall with a crowbar than decorate a cupcake, agreed to join me to celebrate our 60th birthday year. For about $250 each, we could spend three nights in the elderly city less than a day's drive from home. My funk dissolved as I researched B&B's and brushed up on my French. Already I had begun to participate in the weekly French Table at my college, and encouraged by the French professor's compliments on my accent, conversed a little more each week. By the time I found a reasonable B&B in Québec within walking distance of the Old City, I dared to confirm the reservations *en français.*

I passed through the Porte St. Louis into the Old City of Québec, fingering my purse and my stiff, new passport, 42 years in the making, and I wept. Okay, call me foolishly romantic. I don't mind. Elegant 17th century stone buildings, like Cinderella's castle etched a fairytale skyline; horses drawing the *calèches* clop-clopped a counterpoint to the musical murmur of French; strains of accordion music, muted sax, an aching violin floated into the evening air amidst the gentle clatter of cutlery and conversation in street side cafes. Flowers bloomed everywhere. Most extraordinary, fresh lace curtains hung in many of the windows of these centuries-old stone buildings. "Carol! Somebody *lives* in there!" These weathered stone buildings, so gracefully decorated by the women within them, gave me a new spin on elder femininity. *Everything so old – and so beautiful! Stay vital. Stay visible. Stay pretty.*

Our second day, Carol and I poked around Basse Ville, a cheery warren of boutiques crammed into alleyways, and decided to split up for a while. Folk fiddling drew me to a small plaza where a man in fisherman's cap sat and played while his feet clacked a hornpipe rhythm on a board. The small group of onlookers clapped politely and dispersed. Between tunes, I approached him.

"*Merci bien*! Thank you! I dance to music like that in the States … but not here."

"And why not dance here?"

"Er, well, I don't have a partner."

Without a word, the man placed his fiddle in its case and flipped on a CD player. As a fiddle reel began to throb, he approached me, arms lifted in ballroom position. Who am I to waste a dance?

My nameless partner and I effortlessly matched each other's rhythms and danced a reel in morning sunshine on the cobblestones. A passing Asian tour group paused to whip out cameras, laugh, and applaud our performance. Carol missed the whole thing but knows I did it. My kids later admitted being unsettled by my postcard: "*LOVE Québec City! I've been dancing in the street!*"

I still ponder my visit. The graceful Vieux-Québec (Old City), affectionately known as "la belle Grande Dame" retains her charms well into old age. Perhaps I can, too. *This year, Québec City. Next year I'll revel in the romance of Paris!* But the following year those reveling in romance were my youngest daughter and her beloved who popped the question over Labor Day. No, the next year I would celebrate a wedding, not Paris.

Now, this Christmas, I finally have the plane ticket. Do I still have the nerve? ###

Chapter 2
Bon Courage! Hang in There!

As soon as you trust yourself, you will know how to live. –
Johann Wolfgang von Goethe

I drape the red pashmina scarf over my shoulders, loop a knot -- and look strangled. Will I ever wear a scarf with panache? My colleagues have surprised me with a bon voyage party and gifts with a French theme: red roses, a red Pashmina shawl, and crocheted beret in a French hatbox. *Mon Dieu!* They actually believe my madness! They actually believe that I am going to France! Why can't I? My son, friends, and so many others are wildly happy for me. I cannot let them down. I must make this trip and rebuild my ragged self-confidence.

Two months before my departure, however, my courage falters. France? Alone? At my age? A litany of catastrophe drones in my head: Bedbugs. Pickpockets. Roundabouts with manic French drivers. Gas stoves. Muggers at the ATM's. Good God, even a volcano erupting in Iceland raises havoc with European travel. What was I thinking? Wouldn't it be easier just to read the books, stare at the scenic calendars? And how will I pay? World traveler Mon Cher assures me it's just pre-travel jitters. Nonetheless, I discreetly investigate penalties for canceling or shortening the trip, only to discover that my son would lose a fortune;

my son, who seethes that I've been treated so unprofessionally and admires that I have walked away.

Word gets out that I've quit my part-time job, that I'll go to France for a month when my courses end. Friends with benefitted fulltime jobs sigh: "You're so brave!" I demur. Quite simply, desperation is a great motivator, and I desperately want to see Paris before I die. Like the coyote that will chew his foot off to escape a trap, I, too, pay a high price for my freedom: a 60% pay cut.

The very next day I back into a red Saab. It shouldn't have been parked exactly opposite my driveway in the first place, but I'm at fault. Dirty window? Sun glare? Stress? I call the police and wait, my self-confidence shrinking by the moment. *Why couldn't I see the car? It was red, after all! I missed it this morning, why not now? How can I trust myself anymore? Old people have accidents.*

The car's owner, a therapist about my age, arrives before the police officer. She seems philosophical about the smashed headlight and thanks me profusely for not driving away. We finish the paperwork, and I pull back into the driveway, return to my apartment, and turn to jelly. How can I travel to Paris if I can't even back out of my driveway?

Two weeks later, I nearly back into a car at the grocery store. Am I losing my mind or is this inattention a temporary condition? How can I become as brave as friends think I already am? What does it cost to ransom my self-confidence? Where is it hiding?

I certainly wasn't born brave, but I may have inherited the genes for it. After all, Dad fought in the U.S. Army's 10th

Mountain Division in the Italian Alps, and city-bred Mom taught all eight grades in a one-room country school. Timid me, on the other hand, cried at loud and sudden noises: balloons popping, fireworks, sirens. I recoiled at strangers; I hid under the bed when company arrived. I got homesick at sleepovers, even at my cousin's.

Perhaps we always stretch our boundaries first in our minds, and once we're stretched, we never quite return to our original shape. Perhaps like learning the alphabet, we acquire courage a tiny bit at a time and never, ever forget it.

When I was very small, perhaps five or six years old, my mother would sometimes pack peanut butter and jelly sandwiches, tomatoes from the garden, and milk in a Mason jar, then lead my brother and me to The Picnic Tree, a large pine a couple of hundred yards from our isolated New Hampshire home. There we'd eat our lunch, lulled by the resin-scented breeze, safe under those sheltering boughs. Our footfall made no noise on the brown pine needles; cicadas whirred like mechanical wind-up insects.

The security of our idyllic setting and Mother's presence inspired me to dare myself to jump off The Rock. This granite boulder with an angled top probably measured a meter high, but to a little person who needed toe holds to reach the summit, the drop looked treacherous. For the first few jumps, my mother held my hand. Then, emboldened and encouraged by my small success, I crouched and sprung with no help, landed on both feet, exhilarated – a few neurons braver than before.

Some 35 years later, I hiked to 11,300 feet to cover a story on acid rain studies. Had jumping off the Picnic Tree rock prepared me for this? No matter that the wind blew me off balance and I fell, telephoto lens first, into a boulder. No matter that I banged up my knee because I couldn't break my fall. My hydrologist companion with a broken toe and I limped eight miles to the trailhead. Our hobbled progress took an extra hour, but we talked and sang old radio commercials for Oscar Mayer wieners and Mayflower Movers and silly jingles to pass the time. We gave ourselves high marks for admirable expedition behavior.

Living for years in the Wyoming home of the National Outdoor Leadership School (NOLS), I had learned from friends who were course instructors about "expedition behavior," that is, maintaining a positive outlook for the good of the group. I also had met truly intrepid outdoor people whose travels exposed them to dangers greater than pickpockets, for example, Stacy Allison, the first American woman to summit Mount Everest. I had interviewed Stacy when I was a journalist covering a NOLS conference. A diminutive woman with plastic barrettes in her hair, Stacy looked more like a kindergarten teacher than a mountain climber who had crossed the Khumbu Ice Fall on a ladder that could be sucked into oblivion if a crevasse split open. Most of all, I remember her saying, "Trust yourself or nobody else will." It became my mantra.

Hadn't I posted those words over my desk to help me to be strong for the kids when child support dried up? Hadn't I learned to skin antelope and sing for funerals and decorate cakes to eke out my meager income? Back then, caving in wasn't an option. Back then, I had to be strong for my children. Now I have to be strong for me – and the friends who say, "I wish I had your nerve."

My quaking confidence peeks from its foxhole as I recall other times I redeemed it, like the dining room disaster at a Professional Golf Association resort when I was 21 and working as a server. Shouldering my tray with my right hand, I'd swing open the door to the dining room with my left. I must have tripped to launch that tray like a javelin toward the table of six near the door. When I looked up from the floor and saw sour cream sliding down a bald head, I freaked out, ran crying back into the kitchen, and hid behind the icemaker. The *maître d'* and hostess pulled me out, gave me, then a teetotaler, a shot of brandy, and sat me down in an alcove.

"Sugar," she said, "You gotta go back. You gotta finish, otherwise you'll always be afraid. When you fall offa that horse, you get right back on!"

All the other 20-somethings snuck in to give me encouragement. That lovely girl from the South drawled about the time she dropped a whole turkey – splat! – right in the middle of a table. Another confided about tilting a sizzling filet into her guest's lap. Every server had endured a now-hilarious catastrophe. So, I wiped away tears and brandy fumes and finished my shift before I had the rest of the day off.

The next morning still jittery as I set up for breakfast, I dropped a small tray of maple syrup pitchers. Aside from sticky sneakers, I carried on. Later, after guests had left, I dropped a tray of silverware. No biggie. I carried on and curiously, never dropped anything else. I found myself relaxing for I had conquered two fears, not just one: The bald man, the lecherous bandleader, who took the brunt of the tray and sour cream no longer made daily passes at me. From then on, he left me alone.

Refreshed confidence flickers into enough energy that I can now make decisions, and a long-buried possibility rises. In a doctor's waiting room ten years ago, I had read an article praising lodging in European convents and monasteries as safe, quiet, simple, and cheap. Of course! Within a few weeks, I track down a monastery on Corsica offering very inexpensive rooms and meals and book a 5-day retreat, complete with ferry crossing and taxi. I find similar no-frills lodging at the *Sacré Coeur* guesthouse in Paris and at the *hotêlerie* beside Chartres Cathedral. Now both holy places and people with friendly faces anchor my trip. I continue to plot the solitary parts of my journey to stretch between these more secure places where I'll find someone who expects me, who knows my name.

With only two months now until I depart, I must eliminate unknowns that generate fears. I revisit my litany of catastrophe.

Pickpockets! One friend lends me a money belt. Another gives me a purse with multiple fasteners even I can't open in a hurry. I read travel blogs and take heed from the story of a thief and older traveler at ATM's in Paris. Watch your back. Don't be a target. Don't flash the guidebooks or maps.

For goodness sakes, don't look like a tourist. Blend in. Perhaps my new scarf will help.

Bedbugs! Pack a thin plastic poncho to sleep on, if necessary.

Gas Stove! Take advice from globetrotter Marci: *"Skip it. Eat salads. Drink wine."*

Driving! Trust my maps, my wits, and the knowledge that if I die, my obituary will name an exotic locale.

Money! Get a credit card. The trip requires only half the credit line. Set a daily allowance, and pay it off like a mortgage or student loan – heaven knows this will be an educational experience. Besides, I need to go *now* while I can still walk, climb, and see.

Volcano! Seriously, now. After waiting 40 years for my trip, what are the odds of being annihilated by a volcano in Iceland? If my flight is actually cancelled and I'm trapped in France … *"Trapped* in France"? *Pas de problème.*

Yes, I can do this. Of course, I can do this. I head to the attic to find my suitcase, the little black one. ###

Chapter 3
The Journey Begins

*"Twenty years from now you will be more disappointed by
the things that you didn't do than by the ones you did do. So
throw off the bowlines. Sail away from the safe harbor. Catch the
trade winds in your sails. Explore. Dream. Discover."*
– Mark Twain

The week before I leave, Tom sends me a Toulouse-
Lautrec notecard: *At the Moulin Rouge, the Dance.* I
chuckle at the middle-aged woman in red stockings who
dances with enough abandon to clear the floor, while prim
onlookers in bustles and feathered hats radiate disapproval
– or envy.

Oh Mumsy,

*I'm anxious, excited, ecstatic, and proud of you to be beginning
this journey. Traveling has become for me a force in shaping my
memories, my sense of place, and all of my future goals, and I'm
moved that you've found my efforts to kick-start your own moves
so moving. But of course, the brain and heart I bring to my tropical
haunts has "MADE BY MUMSY" stamped all over them; the
eyes I bring are keener, too, knowing you'll be expecting good
stories upon my return. So please go spy a few tall tales for me.
And take a cue from our cover gal and kick up your heels while
you're at it.*

Love, Tom

And to think I even considered not going, letting him down …

The afternoon I leave, I find a "Goodbye and Good luck" card on the kitchen table from my darling, Mon Cher who will housesit for me while I travel. He writes that I will come back "changed." He writes that the plane that takes me away carries "precious cargo" … I am precious … Hold that thought. *I am precious ...*

Just a year ago, Mon Cher burst into my life like a meteor, dazzling - and trailing emotional debris in his wake. With but a stroke of his finger, he brought me back to life. For 22 years after my divorce, Passion had passed me by, not surprising since I invested all my energy in survival, raising four kiddos alone. I was a package deal, and men my age wisely shied away. Living in Wyoming, the least populous state in the union no doubt limited my prospects. Only benevolent uncle types 15 years older seemed interested in me. These gallant gentlemen wanted to rescue me, but I did not want to be rescued.

Then when my youngest child graduated from high school and moved into her own nest, mine became officially Empty. Most evenings I curled up with the cat and a good library book, resigned to living my life for my children, my elderly parents, my students, my church family, my cat, and my African violets. A few worthy activities, a few social dances, a few daydreams, *Someday I will go to France … someday …* rounded out a simple life.

Then one spring morning at church coffee hour, the stranger caught my eye: black turtleneck, black jeans, silver bracelet, and silvery hair drawn back in a ponytail, silver beard. His perfect teeth, tan face, and broad chest, suggested vitality. Virility.

As he talked with the folks involved with the Jamaica Mission, I sidled over in time to hear him say, "… I taught English on St. Thomas for 25 years …"

"I teach English, too!" I blurted, perhaps the most benefit I'd ever wrung out of my college major. He smiled a slow, tilting smile that made his eyes crinkle, and we began to talk.

We talked coffee hour into lunch and talked lunch into a long walk around this quaint New Hampshire town, his boyhood home. Five hours later, he walked me to my apartment, where I was too nervous to invite him in. You just never know about strangers.

"I fly back to Asheville in three days to teach summer school," he said. "Would you like to go out for dinner tomorrow night?"

"Well, I'd really love to, but I have to go to chorale. I missed today."

"How about the next night?"

"Um, actually, I have to take the cat to the vet at 5." *Maybe he thinks I'm making excuses.*

"How about right after that? Say, 6?" *Another chance!*

"Yes … yes, I'd like that."

He smiled and stroked my forearm with his index finger. Like a child enchanted by her first soap bubbles, I fixated on those muscular hands, that chunky silver bracelet, that smile. Suddenly, he kissed my cheek, my first kiss in 15 years. I felt hot, terribly hot, and lightheaded. *Breathe! Keep breathing!*

We said many goodbyes and, finally, he walked away looking back a couple of times to nod and wave. I remained frozen to the porch stair, heart pounding, sweating, shallowly breathing as though I'd gone into a skid and just missed plunging into a canyon. *Maybe I'm too old for this …*

Our dinner date lasted until the waiters stacked chairs on the tables. This time, once we reached my apartment, I dared to invite him in. Much more talk. By 1 a.m., he began to head for the door, pausing every few feet for another cautious kiss. He promised to keep in touch. *Will you? Just in case, I need to remember this.* I cupped his face in my hands, tried to memorize his eyes, and kissed his nose. Then he was gone.

True to his word, he emailed me within two days and continued to write, both email and greeting cards, nearly every day. Now here's another card … *precious cargo …*

On the way to the bus station, I have allowed just enough time to go to the bank to exchange my wad of gift dollars, from him, the kids, and my piggy bank for euros. The bank lady says, "No. We need two to three days." Days. And my bus leaves in 45 minutes. *Pas de problème.* I'll just exchange them in France.

Mon Cher and I have decided that there's no point in his driving to the Boston airport, especially at rush hour. Besides, he's sick. At the bus station, Mon Cher says goodbye several times, kisses several times. Hug. Smack.

Allons-y! Let's go! I board after the silver-haired woman wearing an Indian skirt and sandals, a guitar strapped on her back. Hiking boots dangle from her backpack. I'm a pansy compared with this intrepid explorer. I settle into a window seat. Deep breath. *I am on my way to France! To Paris! To Professor Tapscott's place!* The bus heaves toward the Interstate on-ramp. *The key!* I've forgotten the key to his house in Languedoc. Just when I thought I had cleared my mind ... It was on the bed ... Must have slid under the blanket at the foot of it ... *Get off the bus? Don't panic. You can't panic ... Mon Cher can mail it. Yes, Mon Cher can mail it. Call Mon Cher. Now. He'll be home. And I wasn't going to bring my flip phone ... Deadweight in Europe ... Thank goodness I have my phone ...*

"No key, Sweetie? Let me check. White envelope, huh? ... Yup. Here it is. Hey, Honey, not to worry. My Mom used to send things to me in New York by bus all the time. Let me check the bus schedule ... Yup ... There's another one before your flight. I'll send the key down by bus, OK? Hey, Sweetie, don't worry."

But worries swarm like weevils through my thoughts. Wouldn't mail be better? What if I can't find the bus? What if the bus gets stuck in traffic? Whatifwhatifwhatif ...

"... It's going to be fine. I'll call the bus station and call you back ..."

The bus streaks down I-93. On the side of the highway I see all kinds of emergency equipment flashing red and blue – and black skid marks. Dear God! Three crushed vehicles, one upside down and flat. Horrible. I look away. Travel is not without its perils. A pilgrimage, if that's what this journey is, is not without raw moments demanding faith in myself, in others, and in God. I say quick prayers for the victims, the helpers.

The phone vibrates against my thigh. Mon Cher. "I can put this on the next bus. Just wait outside for the bus driver and bus number 609. OK? Just be outside. Love you."

OK. I can do this. Worries about aging buzz in my mind. *I'm forgetful. I'm confused.* I swat at these pesky thoughts like at so many mosquitoes. *All I did was forget something that was hidden anyway. I CAN do this! Pas de problème ...* Say it again: *PAS DE PROBLÈME!*

Good girl.

The Boston skyline looks familiar, but the international terminal of Logan does not. Here the journey, the adventure into the unknown begins. I lumber off the bus with my shoulder bag, fetch my suitcase, then look around for open ticket counters for Iceland Air. None. Of course. It's only 5 o'clock and my flight leaves at 9:30 p.m. Plenty of time to figure it out.

I bump into a dear colleague who accompanies an Albanian woman with a child and a trolley full of baggage, child's car seat and all. She's moving for a year. Due to Eyjafjallajökull, the volcano erupting in Iceland, her friend's flight to Albania is delayed until Saturday. It is now Tuesday. They await a friend with a truck and who will store this mound of luggage for the week. My shoulder bag is a mere trifle compared to this woman's load. So far, the volcano has not affected me.

My son Tom, who attends college in Boston, wants to see me off. Once he arrives, we watch the clock to anticipate the bus with the professor's key. By 6:15 p.m. we plant ourselves outside amid the roar of traffic, diesel fumes, and cigarette smoke. From our vantage point, we see all traffic sweep a curve before approaching the terminal. Tom thinks the bus will stop on the lower level. I insist that the bus driver said, "here." At 6:35 p.m. the bus arrives about 100 yards away, blocked by traffic directly in front of us. Tom races to the bus, speaks to the driver. By the time I get to the bus, Tom has a manila envelope. Yes! The bus driver says, "I'm not supposed to be on this level, but I didn't see you downstairs." Divine intervention? I stash the key, an old fashioned, metal affair about four inches long, in the middle pouch of my impenetrable travel purse where I will hug it against my belly for the next 12 days.

Tom and I have a sandwich, and he snaps a photo of me. Dreadful. I certainly don't look as excited and youthful as I feel, rather like the heady delusion a day after giving birth. Photos never revealed the exhilarated feeling, only the washed out, still bloated woman who needed sleep.

By 8 p.m., hordes of travelers have already crowded into the security checkpoint. Tom gives me an extra-long squeeze and disappears. Now I'm funneled through a dense pack of travelers who speak guttural languages, and I discreetly read passports covers to know where they're from. Now open the computer case. Off with the purse, the shoes, the money belt. How? The male attendant deftly unsnaps it. We travelers obediently follow directions, lines, like sheep being herded to the dip tank.

Takeoff. Cruising altitude. Then lulled by the nothingness of the black Atlantic, I sleep.

I awaken 4,000 miles from the man who calls me "precious," where no one knows me but God, and where I know only one word – *tåk* – thank you. Grateful, beloved, and infinitely curious, I venture into the unknown. ###

Chapter 4
A Kindred Spirit in Iceland

Ensam är stark. Alone is strong. – *Swedish proverb*

My watch reads 1:30 a.m. as we descend into grey Reykjavik misty with rain. Local time, 6:30 a.m. Perhaps we have landed on Iceland's satellite moon, for I see only a 360° sweep of silvery pale horizon under lowering cloud. No traffic disturbs the perfect quiet. I see no nearby buildings save the airport, a glass and chrome study in lean Scandinavian design as impersonal and cool as a Sci-Fi movie set.

The flight attendants, fair as moonstones, wish us *bless,* an apt goodbye. I respond, *tåk,* thanks, and feel ridiculously clever, or more likely, dazed by jetlag. Ours seems to be the only flight in the echoing terminal. I follow the herd of travelers toward my first customs entry where a jowly man in a high booth takes my passport, frowns, then stamps it without comment.

Now I must find my hostel some miles away. First, water. I am dehydrating. I wander through the duty-free shop and pick up a plastic bottle of clear liquid but cannot read the Icelandic label. Cost, four digits. I have no Kroner, but my credit card works. The first fizzy sip startles me. I have bought sparkling water, refreshing, nonetheless.

I find my way to the tour-sized coach, the first leg to Reykjavik. A jovial driver, lean with grizzled red and grey beard like van Gogh, swings my suitcase into the hold and gestures me inside. I find a window seat and draw back the thick curtains. I want to see everything. Soon, we cruise along highways so perfectly clean and fresh they look like PlaySkool™ toys; only the little wooden cars are missing. For 20-30 minutes, we drive past only an occasional vehicle. Low rock encrusted with lichen sweeps inland as far as I can see on my right. On my left, the vast midnight blue expanse of the Atlantic spreads to the horizon. All houses seem to be made of stone or concrete, not surprising as I have yet to see a tree. Only when we arrive in Reykjavik do I see any vegetation, mostly larch trees and daffodils. The small homes are lovingly landscaped and have a surprising number of swing sets.

We arrive at a bus terminal where I am now directed to a shuttle-type bus and another very jovial bus driver. "First trip to Iceland?" Yes. "It's God's country!" Where am I from? The USA? "Well, you finally have a good President, huh! That George W. Bush ..." He grumbles briefly and wags his head, then resumes his cheerful demeanor and pulls up in front of my lodgings on the edge of Reykjavik. Green lawns surround the plain stucco building near a small traffic rotary. Sulfurous steam rises from the adjacent geothermal community pool. I lug my baggage and try to maneuver the door. Push? Pull? I have arrived but cannot get in. This will become a metaphor for my journey.

The 30-something desk clerk with dark rimmed glasses, buzzes me in, and greets me with a smile and pleasant chat about my travel. Since my room isn't yet ready, we hatch a plan. I'll eat breakfast today instead of tomorrow when I'll miss it by leaving so early, stow my bags in the luggage room, and explore until the room becomes ready mid-day.

The aroma of toast and coffee plus the hum of conversation draw me to the dining room where long wooden tables overlook a swath of lawn visible through patio doors. Abstract plastic mobiles in neon colors add a bit of fun to the space, cozy as a den. A few other guests eat alone or in pairs. All seem to be waking and deep in their own thoughts. All are dressed for a rugged day outdoors.

I find dishes and flatware, then survey the spread, a real *Smörgasbord*: a platter of salted meats (ham, sausage, mortadella); several hard cheeses; granolas; milk; yogurt cups; fruit bowl; fruit compote; a strange barley mixture with apples, raisins, and cinnamon; bagels, rusks, rolls, and those sweet "digestive biscuits" I adore; juices, teas, and Viking-strength coffee, the last large cup I would see for weeks. Here I learn my first travel lesson: Eat a massive breakfast when it's offered. Who knows how my day and access to food will unfold? The adjacent lounge offers computers and Wi-Fi connections, so I shoot off my first email on my tiny laptop. My children have insisted I check in often. Now to explore.

Though I had planned to refresh myself in the Blue Lagoon, I can't face another long bus ride, especially one back the way I just came. Instead, I head downtown and walk a great deal of the city proper, energized by the minty clean air. Passersby, a number with pram-style baby carriages, not the jogger type, give directions in good English and with great kindness.

Quite by accident, I wander close to Hallgrímskirkja, a modernistic church that cascades from the top of the steeple to the earth in lava-like ripples of stone. The massive door is unlocked, so I wander in and find myself alone in a vast, pale space that draws my eyes upward maybe 200 feet. An organ rehearsal is in progress. I sit in a pew in the back and absorb the sound, the light, and the nameless peace I often find in beautiful churches. This benign space lulls me, but I must keep moving before I fall asleep.

Outside, I find a statue of Leif Erikson close by. Signs tell me that he was here first and bears no connection to the church; both simply share the summit of this hill. As I consider this Nordic explorer from a thousand years ago, I think of my plucky Swedish grandmother, Hannah Bernadina Elizabeth affectionately known as "Alice."

About 100 years ago, my grandmother settled in a New Hampshire mill town, where other family members were already established. I wonder what motivated Grammy to emigrate from her native Göteborg, Sweden, to the United States, alone, at age 14. The push of desperation? The pull of optimism? *What's over there? Let's go look ...*

She married another Swede, had four boys, and worked in the textile mills. How she managed to raise her family after her husband died when Dad was only seven, I'll never know. I do know that when I was a single Mom raising four children in Wyoming, I often channeled her grit and reasoned, "If Grammy could raise four kids alone, I can do it, too!" Her example inspired me to be strong.

Independent and fiercely herself, Grammy chopped firewood to feed the pot-bellied stove and fried potatoes with pork chops for breakfast. She tended a huge vegetable garden beside her two-room house. I remember its heavy, musty smell of wood smoke and dampness, cracked linoleum, her little bedside clock ticking on an embroidered cloth, draperies instead of doors separating two rooms. And no bathroom. I never did visit the outhouse.

Grammy was the genuine article with no need to please. Totally lacking vanity, she patted flour on her face. "Same as powder," she insisted. Occasionally she tolerated some grooming at the hands of Aunty Peggy, like before my eighth-grade graduation. The family beautician could, if she had a chance, remove embarrassing chin hairs and wrench Grammy's iron-gray bob into curls with a permanent.

My grandmother smelled of wood smoke those Sundays Dad would pick her up and bring her to our house for dinner. Together, we'd do crossword contests – no small feat for someone who spoke English as a second language. I remember her puzzling over one choice: "How to quiet a child? A ruse or a rusk?" She looked at me with those faraway, ice-blue eyes deeply lined and framed by Woolworth's eyeglasses, the pale beige frames held together with a safety pin. We made our best guess then sent our entry. Grammy always hoped she'd win the prize money, but she never did.

One time, she offered a Swedish blessing over the food. I liked the lilting cadence, like a happy dance. When I begged to learn a few words in Swedish, she became impatient with what I heard as "aww" "eh" and "err." I could not pronounce what I later learned were å, ä, ö. Grammy had trouble with names and called me "the girl," my brother "the baby," and my mother, "the lady." Even as a child, I found this odd and vaguely unsettling, perhaps because I wished for a connection with this strange woman who was related to me.

Back then, how I wished she could have been a pink and white spun sugar kind of grandmother. Instead, my Grammy walked with a swinging gait in her worn down heels and ugly ochre cotton stockings. Her lopsided black or navy dress often showed a drooping slip or an escaping corset strap. Carrying her black oilcloth satchel with a can of worms and fishing rod, she'd walk more than a mile to Lake Massabesic to fish. Then one day when I was 14, and she was 75, she dropped dead, apparently while loading logs into the woodstove.

Now that I'm almost Grammy's age myself, I better appreciate her resilience, her strong sense of self. Perhaps her daring permeates my DNA and will inspire my journey. Leif Erickson and Grammy remind me, that I, too, am strong. Like them, I can risk venturing beyond my boundaries.

Flagging from only four hours of sleep in the past 48, I abandon my quest for Icelandic yarn. Though I find a woolen shop, I'm too whacked to make a decision or walk any farther, so I opt for a city bus back to the hostel. I easily find the main terminal, but the clerk refuses to sell me a ticket, about $1.30, unless I have Kroner. He accepts neither US coins nor credit cards. I must change my currency. Resigned to this detour, I walk to the bank across the street, take a number, and wait with half a dozen other customers. I nearly miss my chance because I cannot understand the numbers being called in Icelandic. Only the digital display alerts me to my turn. Riding the bus back to the hostel, I carry a half-pound of extra coins because I had no small bills to exchange. Sunshine now breaks through the gloom, and I give myself high marks for navigating alone all day with an Icelandic vocabulary limited to two words: thank you and goodbye.

By the time I flop into bed, I've forgotten what day it is. Time is meaningless. Sleep settles over me like a silken shawl. I wake before my 4 a.m. alarm to the deep breathing of my five female roommates, and distant birdsong. Pearly pink Arctic glow lights the dorm. No one wakes or even shifts when I click the door closed and roll my suitcase away. No one here knows I exist.

Though the Reykjavik airport seemed empty when I arrived so early yesterday morning, now it is surprisingly jammed. Two lovers in wooly hats prepare to separate. She holds him in a tight embrace and kisses him again and again. He stands like a post with his hands in his pockets. Why do I think of Mon Cher?

On the plane, I sit by the window next to a pleasant middle-aged couple, fair with smile wrinkles. They read books whose titles appear to be in Icelandic. We don't talk. Shortly after takeoff, I see dense black clouds below and realize it's smoke billowing from the volcano at Eyjafjallajökull. I cannot contain my excitement and tap my seatmate who stretches to catch the view. Now she seems pleased to chat about the volcano and our trips. She and her husband are off to Paris for an anniversary weekend. As I describe waiting 40 years for this trip to Paris, she smiles more broadly and applauds my journey. I return to cloud watching. About an hour out of Paris, my seatmate orders a small bottle of champagne. Surprise! She offers to share it not with her husband, but with me.

"*Skál!*" Cheers! She toasts. "For your special trip!"

"Skál," *to you, Grammy.* "Tåk." ###

Chapter 5
A Red Rubber Nose in Paris

It's no use going back to yesterday, because
I was a different person then.
– Lewis Carroll, *Alice in Wonderland*

I awake to pastel sky and birdsong. Pigeons coo and swoop over the rose tree budding on the balcony outside my French doors. A grassy courtyard separates me from the eight-story apartment opposite, its balconies crammed with tiny tables and chairs, more roses, vines, even potted trees. I gaze upon something pretty everywhere. Contented as a cat, I snuggle deeper into my many pillows, trying to remind myself that I am actually here at my B&B in Paris. I arrived late yesterday afternoon.

I could not open the door.

I buzz. "Hélène, it's Gail! From the United States! I'm here!" A flurry of French. She buzzes. I still cannot open the door. Silence. I buzz again. *"Je ne peux pas ouvrir la porte. I can't open the door."* More instructions, slower this time. Another buzz. Aha! A click. I'm in. I pass through a tiny mirror-lined vestibule to the sleek, modern elevator. More doors. More buttons.

In moments, I emerge on the seventh floor just steps to Hélène's door where keys jingle and the lock turns before I can knock. *"Bonjour! Bonjour!"* My hostess gusts into the foyer, a fragrant storm of cheerful welcome and airy kisses.

Her swooping inflection and cadences, her larger than life movements suggest Carol Burnett impersonating a French woman. Not surprising since she is a professional clown and former opera singer. About my age and build, she wears makeup, her auburn hair shaped in a good Sassoon cut – clearly, a woman who takes care of herself.

As I follow her down a short hall to my room, the bright décor reflects her exuberance, each wall a different color: orange, lime, mauve. My room looks exactly as presented online, save a different bedspread. The room is crammed with whimsical clown figurines and carnival-colored art. I blend into the kaleidoscope.

Hélène shows me the water bottles next to my bed. Parched, I open one and pour a glass. She gasps, *"Non, non! Ici!* No, no. Here!"* and moves the glass from a small table to a coaster on the nightstand. Already I have violated protocol. Since a workman is installing pink and yellow day-glo lucite drawer pulls in the kitchen, she serves me tea in the bedroom with instructions not to eat in here … too hard to clean. She shows me the tiny bathroom decorated with colorful posters from musical galas and gestures broadly to the left side of the sink jammed with dozens of perfume bottles and glass jars of cosmetics. In careful English she tells me, "This is ME." She gestures to the empty right side, "This is YOU." No ambiguity here.

Hélène gives me my key with a rhinestone fob, guidebooks, and business cards to nearby restaurants. She tells me that Nieli Ristorante, the Italian place, is quite good, that she sends many guests there. Tonight, she will be going to the opera and will be back after 11 p.m. She bids me good evening. I am on my own – and pray I can open the downstairs door without her coaching.

Once outside, I wander through the nearby park dense with leafy alcoves for women conversing on benches, for toddlers playing in a sandbox. The tree-lined streets here are short and not parallel with each other, so I make an effort to remember landmarks: St. Joan of Arc Church, a greengrocer, a patisserie. By 6 p.m., jet lag trumps my curiosity. It's time for an early dinner and bed, so I stroll to the Italian place a few blocks from the B&B only to find it closed. Perhaps today is a holiday.

An Asian woman walking a beautiful Golden Retriever smiles, and when I praise her dog, she pauses to talk. I comment about the closed restaurant and she tells me that it's not a holiday, it's just too early. Restaurants open at 7 p.m. I continue exploring until 7, then return to the restaurant where the *maître'd* graciously welcomes me and seats me in the center of the empty dining room at a tiny table facing the door.

Young lovers, who seem to be regulars, arrive in a flurry of conversation and hand gestures. Though I cannot hear their words, I can hear the excited cadences of their impassioned speech. More intriguing is the little white mop of a dog with a pink bow on her head, whom the man addresses as "Babette." The dog, perhaps a West Highland terrier, curls up under the table and promptly goes to sleep. I savor the dark wood and etched glass of this place, my budget ravioli, then silently toast my arrival in Paris with the house red: "*Salut*! To women *d'un certain âge,* wherever you are!"

Now a low murmur of radio voices and coffee aroma tell me Hélène must be up. Last evening, she showed me where my breakfast would be on the kitchen table, so I head there in my jammies. She seems to be at her computer in the next room, but appears at once in the tiny kitchen in her jammies, too.

"*Bonjour*! You have slept well, yes?"

She points out the boiled eggs, the baguette, croissant, juice, and Comté cheese, then teaches me how to make coffee. Imagine! Learning to make French press in Paris. "… and *poussez lentement,* push gently like this." She pours a large cup for each of us and joins me at the table. Since we know enough of each other's languages, we share stories about our children, our lives, our men. When I tell her I was divorced but had met someone last year, she sits bolt upright and claps her hands. When she tells me she had been with a man for five years before breaking it off, she gestures sticking her finger down her throat. Now she has "a friend."

Then Hélène tells how she used to work as a professional clown before enduring an illness and eagerly shows me her clown photo portfolio as *Caneton* (Little Duckling). Her repertoire of expressiveness, manic to wistful, enchants me, so I compliment her.

"Very *dramatique*, no? She glows from the praise.

Perhaps because her dramatic skill needs little embellishment, *Caneton* wears no clown make-up with her satiny yellow costume and gloves, only a red plastic nose. I comment on this and she becomes very serious, and tells about entertaining deathly sick children in hospitals. "The nose, it is *très important,* very important, a barrier to separate reality from the imaginary." I think she means so that her exaggerated faces don't frighten the children – the nose signals that this is make-believe.

So.

What are the red noses in my life? What barriers separate my real world from my imaginary one? Or, by actually sitting in Paris in my butterfly pajamas, have I blurred the line? My fantasy has become real; now that reality takes on a fuller dimension.

After a second cup of coffee, Hélène springs into action. Last evening, she told me to wait on my payment. Now she is all business. I must exchange my dollars for euros. She tells me there is a bank just a couple of blocks away and urges that I complete my mission as soon as possible; she has a full day ahead.

I easily find the bank, which unfortunately does not exchange currency. Hélène will not be pleased. I approach an elderly man ambling along near the *pâtisserie* under the pollarded trees by St. Joan of Arc and inquire in English where to find a bank. He teases me. "English? This is France! We speak French!" So, I repeat in French. Before I can finish, he waves aside my words and continues telling me – in English – that even a certain bank president couldn't exchange dollars for euros at his own bank! He tells me there may be an exchange near Place d'Italie, just a couple of metro stops away.

Hélène seems skeptical, but since she wants her money and needs to go out, she will accompany me, slightly annoyed. I can tell by the sniffs. *Eh bien.* I am learning that her drama is as much a part of her persona as her eye color.

We try a bank that she knows, entering one at a time through a tiny glass vestibule, which closes behind me before it opens in front to let me into the bank. Encapsulated, I expect to be sucked up into the Mother Ship. Hélène and the clerk exchange much agitated French, but the clerk's wagging head does not bode well. She jots some notes then we emerge, one at a time, through the glass bubble and onto the damp street.

Thanks to the clerk, she finds an ATM for me a few blocks away. I withdraw the maximum and pay her in cash. I still need more euros. Now she relaxes and gives me the directions – several times – to the Chinese money exchange in Place d'Italie as by now she thinks I am perhaps mentally deficient. I can't open a door, use a coaster, or bring the right money from home. She departs, and I go on alone.

The Place d'Italie, an intersection of nine streets, some of them major arteries, roars with traffic. With my maps, my adequate French for asking directions, and delights lining all the wrong *rues*, I nose around like a mouse in a maze, starting, reversing, scurrying, pausing, until a lovely young woman in a red scarf with a cello on her back, directs me to rue d'Ivry and the money exchange. A solemn Chinese gentleman takes my cash and my passport and disappears while I wait behind a plate glass window. Bereft of my passport, I dearly hope that this place is legitimate. Eventually he returns with my passport, my euros, and some paperwork, then pleasantly dismisses me.

While I wait for the light to change, a woman approaches and in rapid French asks me for directions. Must be my red scarf. Suddenly my reality shifts: I am no longer a tourist, an outsider. Just as Hélène's red rubber nose distinguishes the imaginary from reality, my red scarf does the same. Yes, I am pretending, but for now, at least, *je suis Parisienne.* ###

Chapter 6
"Paris Will Kiss You"

There is but one Paris. – Vincent Willem van Gogh

My ankles hurt from so much walking over Parisian cobblestones these first few days. I decide to take the Pont-Neuf metro back to the B&B to avoid walking in the rain all the way to the Sully-Morland stop. In the crowded subway car, I sit in the jump-seat by the door. An elegant young couple in black dashes in and leans against the pole. Oblivious of the other passengers, she arches her body into his; he holds her face in his hands. They kiss. Deeply. They are so close I hear their lips part. No one seems to mind, not even the older lady with the grim mouth, when they stumble within inches of her, still embracing and kissing. They kiss, laugh, and kiss some more, then whirl off the train at Place du Châtelet. Kisses in Paris … what could be more perfect? And my thoughts drift to Mon Cher …

He should be here with me, kissing me, instead of back home with my cat. When I emailed him in December about my fabulous Christmas gift and invited him to join me, he jumped at the chance.

"Wow! Let's go now! Why wait 'til May?" When Tom booked my flight, I sent Mon Cher my reservation info, expecting him to find a seat on the same plane right away. A few days later, he emailed me: "… but you're only making a stopover in Reykjavik. Not enough time to see anything, and besides, I've already been to Iceland. I'll just meet you in Paris ..."

In January, we peruse maps together over the phone trying to find the tiny village in Languedoc where I will stay at the professor's place. Yet by the middle of February, Mon Cher still has not booked a flight. It's time to talk. "OK," he sighs on the phone. "I really want to go fishing. It's best in May, and I haven't had a whole month to fish for the past 20 years. Besides, you said you weren't even sure you could swing the trip financially." He pauses. "Hey, how about I give you a chunk of cash to stay in your place while you're gone? It's so close to my fishing spot. And ... and ... I'll take care of Kitty!"

As my departure approaches, Mon Cher offers yet more excuses for not joining me. "This is your Discovery Journey, Sweetie. You'll come back a different woman. You need to do this on your own because you've never traveled. Hey, I'd just be a bag of cement for you to drag around." Each excuse holds a grain of logic. But this trip isn't about logic, it's about romance. Isn't it?

I complain to my writer friend Cathy who reminds me that the original impetus for the trip was a writing sabbatical. "... and if you go with Mon Cher, you won't get nearly as much done. You'll spend too much time, well ... spooning." Perhaps.

Then I complain to my friend Judy. "And here I am going to Paris. Alone. What's Paris without kisses?"

"Paris will kiss you," insists no-nonsense Judy from Brooklyn. "So, go already!"

So, I go. And Mon Cher stays with the cat.

Now as I wander Paris, I glimpse yet more kisses: passionate lovers in public places, like those in the subway, and those awkward kisses on the *vedette*, tour boat, cruise. I smile at the memory.

I had dined alone on salad Niçoise and blonde beer at cozy outdoor Café Louis Philippe, where both privacy fence and arbor were garlanded in red geraniums. As I left, all the waiters bid me *bonsoir.* Such courtesy. No wonder I never feel lonely here. I stroll toward Pont-Neuf to catch the 9 p.m. *vedette* cruise upon the Seine. The upper deck of this boat, which seats at least 300, is partly full, but I spy an empty seat beside the rail as I walk up the gangplank. The throng pushes up the stairs to the upper deck. When someone in line mumbles "Full!" then turns around and descends, many passengers follow. I think, *check it yourself …* and find the seat I had chosen moments ago still waiting for me. Perfect! I pretend that Mon Cher sits in the empty seat beside me.

We begin by cruising west toward the Eiffel Tower, a lacy silhouette against the deepening peach twilight. Surprise! Up close, it's flat Rust-Oleum® brown, not black as I had imagined. Even at 9:00 p.m., it's still light enough to take photos, so the blonde Polish woman behind me obliges. I return the favor. We glide past many other *bateaux;* some carry lively parties that bubble with freshets of laughter. Elegant *bateaux mouches* carry sedate diners and white jacketed waiters. On the candlelit decks of colorful houseboats, clusters of friends drink wine at picnic tables, beside potted tree roses.

Now the *vedette* turns east to cruise the pea soup green Seine. Our guide tells us in French and very good English that our route will take us along the south side of Île de la Cité before we turn back and cruise the north side. I am thrilled to goose bumps, gliding past the images from my calendars – Musée d'Orsay, the Louvre, the Conciergerie. But calendars are silent. These stone-lined banks of the Seine throb with the sounds of humanity in the lingering twilight. Even near 10 p.m., the sun seems reluctant to leave the party.

Everywhere groups of people talk, drink wine, share *les pique-niques*. I am astonished that the impossibly loud drone of conversation on the bank often drowns out the tour guide's voice. Along the banks and under the overpasses jammed with vehicles, African drummers pound here, a jazz ensemble croons there. Farther along the Left Bank, just past the Sorbonne, clusters of people with CD players dance in separate mini-amphitheaters: one group snaps with Apache moves; another waltzes or swings; yet another stomps in line dancing. Now I feel the pulse of this City of Light – and it's racing.

As we turn west toward Île Saint Louis, our guide announces that we will soon pass under the Pont des Arts, "the most romantic bridge in all of Paris." I can't catch why it's so romantic; the blues band on the shore drowns out her voice. Then I hear, "... so we must make a wish as we pass beneath. To make it come true, you must kiss the person next to you!" Twitters of nervous laughter. Always the kisses in Paris!

I regard the 300-lb bulk of the English-speaking man who jammed himself into the seat beside me after the gangplank was raised. He faces the aisle and does not turn or speak to me. Instead, he nods curtly to his wife a few rows back and stiffens his many chins. So much for kisses! I photograph Notre Dame and make a wish, anyway. It includes Mon Cher.

By 9:45 p.m. the light has faded and the *vedette* turns on spotlights that illuminate the undersides of the many bridges as we pass. Just as we return to the Quai de Pont-Neuf, the Eiffel Tower, outlined in still white light, begins to flash with strobe lights, like a disco ball gone wild. After a few minutes, the light again calms to a quiet silhouette against the deepening dusk. I stroll back to the hostel amid throngs of people, deliciously tired and too satisfied to think about kisses.

The next morning, I walk to the Pont des Arts to figure out why our tour guide considers this bridge so romantic. After all, from the *vedette* its slim metal trusses seem minimalistic compared with, say, the lovely Pont Alexandre III, a confection of garlands, gilded statuary, and street lamps entwined with cherubs. As soon as I reach the bridge, I see them: padlocks. So many they glitter like sequins. Thousands of locks scratched or painted with lovers' initials clasp the metal grille fence atop the bridge. The lovers have most likely thrown the keys into the Seine. Padlocks – such concrete emblems of love, quite unlike ephemeral kisses.

So, what is a kiss, anyway? Ultimately closeness. Trust. The security an infant shares with her mother. But a kiss is also sharing of a different sort. Sensuality. Passion. A Perfect Moment.

My college pal Carol taught me about Perfect Moments back when she visited me in my crumbling Boston apartment the year after I dropped out of college. Toward the end of our winter weekend, we sat on the floor of my dingy room, brushed aside fallen ceiling plaster, and listened to Andrés Segovia. Sunlight streamed through the dirty south-facing window. We had pumped the bilge of our murkiest secrets, sharing insecurities, torments, and emerging insights on men.

Carol sighed. "This is perfect." I stared at her. Perfect? Really? Wasn't there always a flaw somewhere? Something missing? How could a moment possibly be *perfect*? Yet, as I considered the icicles dripping into the February afternoon, I recognized the simple pleasure of our lunatic camaraderie, sunlight, and tea, despite the grimy apartment. Carol had introduced me to the notion of the Perfect Moment, and though it has taken many years, I have become an ardent believer.

The following summer, I experienced my first Perfect Moment without Carol's coaching. I had taken a vacation day from my secretarial job to study poetry for a summer school final exam. Early one July afternoon, I lay on the grass in the Harvard Yard, re-reading Wordsworth

.../Trailing clouds of glory do we come/ The sun shone just enough and a fresh breeze rustled the leaves overhead. As I inhaled the moment, I heard "Toccata and Fugue" waft from nearby Memorial Chapel. "Perfect!" I surprised myself with the thought.

I recognize Perfect Moments more frequently now 40 years later, grateful that I can savor in so many ways the delights of my still acute senses. I photograph some of the lovers' locks and wonder vaguely whether Mon Cher and I will ever scratch our initials and click one in place. Once across the bridge, I wander through the Luxembourg Gardens where I gaze upon the loveliness of random roses and cup their softness in my hands to inhale the raspberry sweetness. I listen to the *accordéoniste* stretching and squeezing *"Ciel de Paris"* from his very soul, the cadence of French passersby murmuring around me like a stream. I savor creamy *brebis* on a crusty baguette and a glass of sun-drenched Minervois, red as garnets. *Clung. Clong.* Now the bells of Notre Dame toll the passing minutes, reminding me that eternity is closer than I think. *Clung Clong. Per-fect! Per-fect!*

Caressing my weary senses, moment after Perfect Moment, Paris, indeed, kisses me. ###

Chapter 7
Lille Reunion: A Reflection on Love and Lace

Heart, I said, what a gift it has been
to enter this circle of lovers. – Rumi

Hélène hands me the phone while I'm still eating breakfast. My British friends, Andy and Angela, are delayed crossing the Chunnel from England and will now meet me in Lille around 4:30 p.m., not at noon as planned. Since I already have my train ticket for 10 a.m., I'll go on ahead, explore Lille for a few hours on my own, and check email for their travel updates; I have no European cell phone service. At least I will not expect them to meet me. No worries.

Now more changes as Hélène urges an easier route to Gare du Nord via a new metro station not mentioned in my outdated guidebook. Fortified with many airy kisses, *beaucoup de bisous*, I strike out on the new route. After a brief walk in an unfamiliar area, I easily find the state-of-the-art Bibliothèque Nationale metro stop. The shiny new escalator is out of order, so I heft my heavy suitcase up and down several flights of stairs. Adrenaline neutralizes my aches.

The Gare du Nord station swarms with hundreds of purposeful travelers while the loudspeaker blares incessant announcements to beware pickpockets. Like a high-strung hunting dog, I continuously scan my environment and those close by me. What does a pickpocket look like, anyway? The very high ceiling provides three to four stories of space in the platform area, so I feel less closed in, safer, despite the ominous presence of a soldier in camouflage who aims his automatic rifle at the floor near the glass case of chocolate truffles in ruffled papers.

An oblivious teen cuts the queue as I wait to board. The older gentleman beside me wags his head in disapproval, then gestures for me to enter ahead of him. The teen-in-a-rush turns out to be my seatmate, who graciously hoists my bag onto the lucite shelf overhead before burrowing into his novel.

Once past the industrial fringe of the city, I try to comprehend that this TGV, *Train à Grande Vitesse*, high speed train, flashes over the rails at nearly 200 miles per hour, as though on a cushion of air. Only when we streak past a blur of bushes or scream by a TGV traveling the opposite direction, a Doppler micro-burst next to my face, do I have any true sense of our speed. The scenic route passes through much open land, some just plowed, some already growing green, some fields flowering bright yellow, perhaps in rape or mustard. Serene and sun-warmed, I dissolve into the golden mists of nostalgia and anticipate my reunion with old friends.

Twenty-two years ago, Angela endeared herself to me forever when my washer broke, and she insisted on lugging my full diaper pail about a block to her house to wash and dry the "nappies." A well-traveled flight attendant and French teacher, Angela, and her family from East Anglia, had spent an academic exchange year in our small Wyoming town. Thanks to the "sagebrush telegraph," I anticipated her arrival with fresh muffins, homemade strawberry jam, and an invitation to drop by for coffee.

Within a day or two, she appeared with her daughters, then 5 and 7. Soft-spoken, upbeat, and adventurous, Angela and I hit it off at once. I drove her shopping, to doctor appointments, and to kindergarten events. We babysat for each other. Together we celebrated Thanksgiving, Christmas, children's birthdays, and simple suppers. She easily slid into our neighborhood coffees and book group. Tuesdays Angela gave me French lessons. In so doing, she nurtured not only my fluency and our friendship but also my fragile dreams of travel once diaper days were done.

As my husband's business failed and he sought work elsewhere, as the cracks in my marriage deepened and spread, she listened and gently supported me. A few days before he moved to his native California to take a job, Andy and Angela made dinner for us, the last event we would ever attend as a couple. In my distress, all I remember was their homemade mayonnaise; however, Andy and Angela's stability, wit, and obvious love for each other helped to ease my transition from married to separated. A month after my husband left, Andy and Angela returned to England; by the end of the year, my divorce became final. We kept in contact pretty well for the first ten years, even before the advent of email, then lost touch. Now, after 22 years, we would reunite. What changes might we find in each other? Only four more hours …

Located very close to the Belgian border and the Channel coast, Lille, an industrial center like Manchester, England, dates to medieval times. The baroque Opera and plaza reflecting Flemish influence face one side of the train station, Gare Lille-Flandres. This contrasts sharply with the massive, futuristic EuraLille Shopping Mall facing the other. I trundle my suitcase toward the Old City, find a sunlit café, and enjoy a *croque-monsieur*, an inside out grilled ham and cheese sandwich. To pass some of the afternoon until my friends arrive, I sip *café crème* and amuse myself with my game of Feet and Tongue, watching passersby to guess their language by studying their footwear. My algorithms give me about 80% success rate: Sturdy leather sandals and cross trainers – German; high heels or strappy, colored or metallic sandals – French or Spanish; sneakers, Topsiders, and "walking shoes" – English. Without exception, the women are slim.

By late afternoon, I've had enough stimulation and am ready to wait for my friends in the snugness of my hotel. First, I must find it. Apparently, the Hostel B&B Grand Palais, is not well known since it is so new; furthermore, it is located on the edge of the more modern, industrial part of the city. I wander through the dazzling Mall EuraLille gleaming in magenta lucite and chrome, thinking I will exit on the far side near my hotel. Wrong.

I then I return to the streets, and after walking many blocks, find a Grand Palais Convention Center. Is this it? Flowerbeds full of weeds and locked doors tell me I have no room here, and I feel a stirring of fear. Very few people stroll these sidewalks. A lone man leans against a sycamore and smokes. Should I trust him? Do I have choices? I hatch a plan: confidently approach him but retreat to the mall if he is unhelpful or threatening. The stranger does, indeed, know the way and waves his cigarette toward my destination, *"Là-bas, derrière.* Over there. Two blocks and behind." *Voilà!* Aha! I find the small but efficient hotel, rather like Motel 6, tucked amongst construction sites.

At last! Hugs. Kisses. Angela and I hold each other at arm's length, then embrace again to make sure we aren't mirages. She hasn't aged a day, though Andy's hair has turned silver. They have brought champagne, flutes, and a basket of strawberries, very juicy and sweet, picked in their East Anglian neighborhood – a simple, heartfelt treat. We laugh as the cork pops, then savor the bubbles, millions and millions, that make the wine seem alive, while we talk and share the photo albums, old and new. In theirs, my baby wears diapers; in mine, she wears a wedding gown and veil. I cannot allow myself to think of the intervening years, all that missed time. We have right now and that is enough. A Perfect Moment.

That evening and the next day, we three silver-haired friends ramble through Old Lille in cool spring sunshine, enveloped in conversation, warmed by shared history. I don't remember the food, only the local beer which Andy, the connoisseur, chooses for me from a blue Delft tap. Under canopies of sycamores with new green leaves, past purple lilacs and lavender tulips, we walk and talk. We turn down cobbled streets a mere carriage wide, marveling at the Flemish influence on different doors: ponderous, weathered planks with hand-forged iron latches; polished wood, the windows carved in sinuous designs; faded and flaking teal and ochre doors, gripped by wrought iron reinforcements. What fears, what political realities inspired carpenters to build them to be impenetrable? Could they guess that they would last 500 years? How foolish our glass patio doors seem by comparison. Sleek and gleaming, they afford a view, but no protection whatsoever – a commentary on our more civilized lifestyle or our childlike view of the world?

As the day wears on, I am drawn less to the architecture of Lille and more to the gentle interactions of Andy and Angela who have been married at least 35 years. A love light still gleams in their eyes. When was the last time I observed a beautiful marriage up close?

My friends have spent little time in Lille, so they often refer to maps to negotiate the metro. Andy, the geographer, is in charge of this. Even when they disagree, they never correct each other. Instead, she may preface her opinion, "Perhaps …? Do you suppose …?" He is equally kind. How beautiful to watch their graceful, lifelong *pas de deux*. Like two dancers in a familiar choreography, they anticipate, balance, and trust each other.

Last night during our elegant dinner at Alcide, we enjoyed easy conversation. Neither friend dominated. They easily agreed on the wines. Easy smiles, not just with me, but with each other.

"Here, try some *Waterzoï de Poulet*. What do you suppose *Waterzoï* means?"

"Have a profiterole. I have too many."

"A bit of *mousse au chocolat*? Mmm ...*Merci bien!*"

And so, through the entire meal. The fabric of their marriage is soft and flexible. Like finely knit Merino wool it stretches without chafing and easily returns to shape. My marriage, on the other hand, was more like stiff new denim; it needed a lot of breaking in.

My brilliant former Jesuit and I wed in 1972. June Cleaver had not quite gone, and Gloria Steinem was just emerging. My role seemed unclear. Would I be the agreeable Wifey or the assertive Woman? And though his renounced vows of chastity and obedience dissolved like so much mist, I would soon learn that the vow of poverty was hardwired into his being; practicality overruled aesthetics. And me.

But church bells rang when we opened the gate to our basement apartment just a block from the Atlantic Ocean. Intoxicated by love and the bonus of a slip for the boat – Yes, I bought it for him, so no trip to Europe now – we moved into our nest, smothered in roses. Evenings we sprawled on the kitchen carpet he had installed himself, square by self-adhesive square, avocado and harvest gold so trendy in the 1970s. And by the light of the aquarium, we watched our guppies and mollies. We couldn't afford a TV.

Here I would learn how to share space with someone who gave little thought to possessions. How about his avocado Naugahyde™ swivel chair? Such a find on trash day. Just a few cigarette burns. Or the studio couch that fell open unless propped against a wall? We stuffed the grapefruit-sized hole with scarves. Not what I had envisioned when I perused silver patterns and real china. No. We ate off Melmac™ and chipped oddments from Goodwill. But the bilge pump for the boat? And the Mercedes engine block? These needed to be in the *living room*? Well, sure, we had no garage to work on them. Of course, he could fix them himself. Um, okay. Okay.

To call my new husband Mr. Fix-it would be an understatement. He was more like Gyro Gearloose who spouted Thomas Aquinas. Still, I had envisioned a boudoir of romance, candles, and flowers, not one hung with pegboard, hammers, and pliers. My talented guy used the hulking vise to make our wedding bands. Yes, he needed his creative space, and I got used to dinner guests sniggering when I offered to put their coats on the bed in the "work room." And acquiescence by acquiescence, our new home took shape. I loved my husband's unfettered spirit, which saw "the Big Picture," but our dreams of "home" did not align.

Within two years, Gyro and I moved to a more traditional house, where tools, bilge pump, and engine block never gained entry, though he did use the dishwasher to clean engine parts. Because I *let* him. Like the mouse who rears and thrashes against the eagle's onslaught, I had begun to stand up for my opinions. My assertiveness would continue to grow like a stalagmite, one drop at a time but resolute as stone. Eventually we agreed we had dueling dreams, a.k.a. "irreconcilable differences." He left with his tools; I stayed with four children and a more enlightened attitude toward material things.

Surely, Angela and Andy have had their ups and downs living apart while he taught at a distant college during the week, and she taught close to the home where she raised the girls. Yet, for two independent spirits, a non-traditional arrangement may have been ideal. Space has its charms. And I consider the ubiquitous lace curtains in French windows.

In Québec City, I first discovered that lace curtains signaled life. People, probably women, actually lived inside buildings I thought too ancient to be inhabited. In France, as well, lace curtains abound, the perfect contrast to an old granite or sandstone window casement.

Several small shops sold only lace and afforded me a chance to examine more closely these delicate fabrics composed of hundreds of filaments – some looped, some taut – all surprisingly strong. I learn that laces are created in several ways. Some may be applied to plain ground, an already existing fabric. Some may be painstakingly woven from nothing and stand alone. Yet others are created from solid fabric by removing individual threads, one at a time. What's taken away, thread by thread, then shaped, makes the design. In every lace, no matter the style, empty spaces are essential to loveliness. The allure, the fascination depends upon the chiaroscuro of fiber and shadow, the play of light and dark, of delicate contrast.

So, too, with the network of attachments called love. Like lace, marriage, especially, depends upon predictable spaces entwined in the rhythmic repetition of connections. Unlike the military precision, the regimentation of warp and weft in evenly woven fabric, lace delights the eye with more sinuous, more romantic rhythms. No wonder so many brides choose lace.

And my thoughts drift to Mon Cher so far away. What kind of love lace do we weave, with so many unexpected twists, loops – and knots – in the filaments of our connection? With enough fibers of caring, we have fabric. Without enough, our relationship is just a frayed remnant, a rag.

My old friends touch heads as they read the map together, and I wish I could have what they have: a companion with whom to share decades of personal history. After being single for 22 years, it is something I'll never know, however tightly Mon Cher now weaves himself into what remains of my life. In the meantime, I quietly rejoice that my friends are still so in love.

But enough of love. We must be off. Andy and Angela whisk me to the train station and double-park just long enough for quick kisses and promises to keep in touch. I untangle my purse strap from the seat belt, then dodging traffic, dash from the car, and chance a shortcut to the platform area. Bad idea. The glass-walled vestibule does not connect with the platform. I can see it, but I cannot enter. Worse yet, the door through which I just entered has locked behind me. I am trapped.

Outside, about 20 police cluster, talking. I knock vigorously on the glass and catch the attention of one *gendarme* who opens the door and frowns at me. I try to tell him I want to go to the train station, but he cuts me off and asks if I speak English.

"Well," he tells me, rather unnecessarily, "You should not be in here. The train station is there." He points to the next set of doors.

"*Vous êtes trop gentil.* You are too kind." He does not smile as I escape my glass trap and merge into the swarm of travelers entering the station.

With half an hour before departure, I have plenty of time to check email with a cup of coffee at McDonalds, dependable for Wi-Fi service. Unlike airport gates, French railways post platforms for specific trains just minutes before the train arrives. Shortly before my departure, I close my laptop and grab the case, my purse, my suitcase and … Oh, no! Where's my camera? I quickly check the floor, a chair, the water closet, the service counter. I ask a clerk. No luck. Perhaps it slipped off in Angela's car when I tried to extricate myself from the seat belt. If so, I hope it's on the seat and didn't fall on the pavement. Being locked in the vestibule distracted me, so I never noticed it was missing until now, only 15 minutes before my train.

I try to phone Angela using a public phone and what I thought was a gift phone card, but it does not have enough minutes to call a UK number. Now the departures board flashes that the TGV to Paris boards on platform 5. I can do nothing but board the train. The camera will find me or it will not. I will allow nothing, *but nothing* to spoil my beautiful weekend – or this trip I've dreamed of for 42 years. Strangely calm, I settle into my seat and savor the luxuriant greens as they burst and stream past my window. Already my French spring shows signs of vigorous beginnings and equally vigorous old love. ###

Chapter 8
Chartres Cathedral: Lessons in Endurance and Grace

Faith is not something to grasp; it is something to grow into.
– Mahatma Gandhi

Chartres and its medieval cathedral had not figured in my early itinerary until a librarian at my college urged me to visit "just for the windows." His enthusiasm convinced me to make the easy train trip from Paris en route to Mont-St.-Michel in Normandy. Besides, this pilgrimage site would offer hostel lodging, both safe and budget-friendly.

I see the spires of the cathedral as I leave the train station and ask a passerby, an older woman in wine red jacket, the way to St. Yves Hotêlerie. Pleasant Colette insists upon taking me there. We chat about her flamboyant namesake. She pronounces my name "Guy-EL" and speaks French slowly enough that we can converse. I sense that she wants to talk. Colette enthuses that she likes Americans because they came to help at the end of the war. She still feels gratitude these many years later. I think this is sweet but I have yet to learn the extraordinary story of American "help." My one-person welcoming committee walks me right to the door of my hostel tucked around a wall and down an incline, clearly out of her way. She wishes me good journey and resumes her walk. Her friendliness helps me to feel comfortable right away despite increasing travel fatigue.

I find my white room very clean and fresh with blue shower curtain and blue matelassé bedspread. My "cell" exudes the restful colors of the sky. But rest must wait. I push myself to make a brief tour of the cathedral, including each of the side altars. At the foot of a statue of St. Joseph, I light a votive for Mon Cher and a large candle for a couple back home, something to light their way through his cancer, little knowing he will be dead within the year. Back at the hostel, I flop on the bed, drugged by birdsong and sunshine pouring through tall French windows. Even spread-eagled, I can see the cathedral spires. It's only 5:30 pm, but I am done for today. I eat leftover cheese and bread from my bag, drink water, and take ibuprofen for my hurty knees, then give in to rest. I sleep 14 hours.

The next morning, I wake early. By the time I shower and find the sunny breakfast room, I'm ravenous. Seven euros, about $10, buys me a feast: ham, salami, cheese, yogurt cups, cereal, juices, fresh fruit, baguettes, and croissants. Coffee is served by a machine, and I opt for café crème. The breakfast room is jammed. A leathery man wearing khaki who appears to be traveling alone, makes eye contact with me and jerks his chin toward the empty space across from him. "Help yourself," he says. So, I do. I learn that Jack is from Australia and touring Europe for three months. We converse easily in our shared language. He has already been in the Chartres area for two days. Next stop, the cathedral at Rouen.

"I'm not religious, mind you. But I'm drawn to sacred spaces. Just like to be around 'em."

"Me, too, but just what is it that we feel in them? What draws us?"

Jack drains his tea and stares over my head for a minute. "I think we feel something—prayers, maybe – left by people trying to be good, trying to be their best selves. That positive energy stays there."

I think he's onto something.

Jack continues. "A Yank saved the cathedral, you know."

"Really? How's that?"

"Well, yesterday I was over in Lèves a couple kilometers from here. Found a plaque commemorating a Colonel Griffith. Seems that during World War II, the Yanks and Germans battled here. The Yanks suspected the Germans hid in the cathedral, so an Army commander gave orders to blow it up. This colonel decided to check it out first, even up in the spires. No Germans. None. So, he gets the order rescinded. The cathedral was saved." He pauses, "but later that same day, the poor bloke got shot. Killed."

Both Jack and I fall silent. No wonder Colette likes Americans.

"Well, gotta make tracks. G'day to you. Safe journey." He hefts his beat-up backpack and strides toward his next sacred space. A pilgrim.

Now I step into the grand interior of the cathedral and find a Mass in progress. I slip into one of the many empty chairs in the back. Though I understand little of the rapid French, I follow the chants and hum along. The organ rumbles. Light beams through vermillion and cobalt windows. How many centuries of voices have resounded against this glass and stone? How many good people have prayed here? Jack thinks the goodness remains. Yes, I feel it. I hope I add my few atoms of good will to the place.

After the service, I wander the ambulatory and contemplate the statuary and stained glass, a marvel of human artistry and medieval technology. Flickering votives beside each apse chapel remind me of the human longing here. I have no camera, so I must capture images in my mind. A tour has begun, but I don't join it. Instead, I seek something more than information; a souvenir book can provide that. I need to know why this cathedral has remained relevant for 900 years. Retaining its original glass seems secondary to retaining its purpose. Old is interesting; old and alive, exquisite.

Once the tour busses roll up, the church is no longer a hushed sanctuary for me. It has become a tourist attraction. As I leave, preoccupied with thoughts of beauty, age, and The Good, I walk right past an old man sprawled on the top step. He extends a scallop shell. Another pilgrim. Later, I will remember him, for he has slipped into my head to accompany me on the rest of my journey, silently begging the coin I neglected to give. ###

Chapter 9
Ever Moving Toward the Vision: Mont-Saint-Michel

Do not follow where the path may lead.
Go instead where there is no path and leave a trail.
– Ralph Waldo Emerson

Senior moments or major screw-ups? I'm less than a week into my trip and now, in addition to forgetting the key to the house in Languedoc and letting my camera go to England with Angela, I've botched my connection to Mont-Saint-Michel. Madame at the train station enunciates in French as though for the hard of hearing: "You. Can't. Get. There. From. Here." I was *supposed* to return from Chartres to Gare Montparnasse in Paris and start out again on a northern line. Madame sighs heavily then re-routes me from Chartres through Le Mans and Rennes to Saint-Malo on the Channel coast. She clearly thinks I am an imbecile. Maybe so. Now the dogleg to the Mont becomes fraught with unknowns of pilgrimage proportions. I must trust my mistake-prone self even more – a pilgrimage, indeed.

Already it is 11:00 a.m. My connection leaves at 2:00 p.m. I have time to use the nearby Internet café to reorganize my itinerary, beginning with finding lodging for tonight in Saint-Malo, a city in Brittany, about 45 miles from where I was supposed to be. My guidebook recommends a nice two-star. I quickly find the site for the Nautilus and type my request, but look at the typos! Aha! The French keyboard has tricked me: "q" is "a" and "z" is "w". Hunting and pecking to type the room request squander precious time. I receive no email confirmation of a room before I board the train. Oh well, it's not yet high season. I should be able to find something. I think.

The SNCF local train to Saint-Malo lurches like the Walloping Window Blind, not at all like the sleek TGV that glides effortless over the rails. Since transferring at Le Mans for Rennes, the landscape has become less cultivated, more wild and rolling, dotted with hundreds of cows. I even spy a deer, stopped mid-chew, staring blankly at the passing train.

Few passengers exit at Saint-Malo, but I easily find a taxi driven by a grandfatherly man who speaks no English. He compliments my French during our brief chat while he threads his way within this ancient walled city like Old Québec. He deposits me on the threshold of Hôtel Nautilus. I descend two steps into a snug, wood paneled interior where Friendly Staff greet me, just as the guidebook has promised. But. No room. But. Big smile. Friendly Staff has a friend with a similar two-star hotel, just around the corner. Five minutes' walk. They help each other often. Another big smile. Within 15 minutes, I have checked in at Hotel le Croiseur. My bed is secure. Now, food.

The evening breeze straight off the English Channel invigorates and chills. The cafés have drawn their plastic walls to protect diners. I follow a street that seems to be full of these protected cafés, hoping to stick to my under 9€ budget for a sit-down meal. I find a modest bistro with empty tables and sit in what would have been the street café, except that I am protected by the clear plastic wall facing the street. To get the most protein for my money, I order the *galette de blé noir*, a brown wheat crepe with cooked tomatoes, ham, and egg. Only 5,90€, so I indulge in a Heineken after my topsy-turvy day. Secretly I am glad that I've finally left the trail of my itinerary and begun bushwhacking.

The food satisfies. The beer relaxes. I watch the lean young waiter, maybe 22, who seems to be responsible for tables of eight on the sidewalk. When we make conversation, I tell him I will take the paper placemat with lovely photos of the fort and ramparts as a souvenir because I have lost my camera. He becomes alarmed and says he must first check with his boss. Perhaps he doesn't understand my French and thinks I wanted to take the table ... or dishes ... or flatware as a souvenir. He never checks with his boss because he is out straight with his other tables. I leave the near-frantic guy a tip and tuck the placemat into my purse.

Since it's still light, I walk within the fortress city, past diners protected by clear plastic walls. I hear the pleasant babble of conversation, see them sip their Chablis, crack their lobsters. Everyone is coupled up: the diners, the tourists who stroll hand in hand. The only singleton I meet stands in a doorway, smoking. Perhaps he's a waiter on break. I do not meet his gaze, and when I look down, I notice that the cobblestones are laid in arching patterns, not lines. And I wonder why. Did a long-ago mason yield to a flight of imagination? Or just follow orders? I like to think that perhaps this paver fond of arches acted independently.

By now, I have meandered to the city gate, *la porte*, an archway large enough for cars to drive through. The schooner I spied on my arrival draws my attention, so I migrate toward the harbor, about 200 feet away. Smaller craft rock in the gentle twilight sea. The first, a white dory, bears the name "Surprise" painted in red, an apt metaphor for today's convoluted journey. I laugh out loud, and the gulls laugh with me.

During the night I wake and wonder for a few moments: *Where am I?* I've been traveling now for only a week, but with the exception of Hélène's place in Paris, I've spent only one night in each bed. I calmly remember my location and return to sleep.

The next morning, someone in the bus queue has a timetable. I've at least 15 minutes, time enough to dash into the nearby information bureau to confirm that I'm in the right place. I roll my suitcase and stand behind the elderly woman with the purple roller suitcase, lavender fleece scarf, and lavender jacket. She seems to know exactly where she's headed and confirms, "*Oui! Oui!*" This bus does connect with one to Mont-Saint-Michel. I relax, and we begin to chat. She is heading home to Fougères, the end of the line. Once the bus arrives, she speaks warp speed French with the driver to confirm my transfer. I sit before she does, pat my empty seat, and she joins me.

My companion with the tight gray perm apologizes for her English, so we converse in French for the next 45 minutes or so. She tells me that she is 77 and her name is "Marie-Ange." She says this with a face suggesting she's resigned to it. "Marie Orange?" I ask. She flutters her hands like wings – oh, *angel*. Yes. She smiles and resumes talking in a voice that reminds me of contented doves cooing. How dear! An elderly angel to protect me on my pilgrimage.

Perhaps because I talk about other churches I have already visited – Chartres, Notre Dame, Saint-Germain-des-Prés – she asks if I am Catholic. How to explain without upsetting this dear little French lady from rural Normandy? Just tell the truth. Besides, I'll never see her again ...

"Well, actually I'm Episcopalian, but I was Catholic for 35 years." I think: *My priest was hauled off in handcuffs. My daughter came out of the closet.* I say: "… and then there were, well, difficulties ..."

She pats my hand. "*Oui! Oui! Je comprends!* Yes! Yes! I understand! For me, also, the difficulties! Now...," she glances left and right then whispers her secret. "*Je suis bouddhiste*! I am Buddhist!" We smile broadly at each other, spiritual rebels in accord.

Mon Ange tells me that as a young wife she used to live in Paris in the 15th arrondissement near the Eiffel Tower. Her husband – she rests her cheek on her hands as though sleeping – has been dead nine years. She hasn't been to the United States, but goes to London from time to time. We exchange addresses, and I tell her that she must stay with me when she visits the U.S. She beams a cherubic smile and pumps a fist with her thumb raised. *"D'accord!* OK!"

We converse easily as the bus winds its way through cozy, picturesque villages of stone houses with rose covered arches. Sea breezes sweep the fields flecked with *coquelicots*, poppies, scattered like dandelions. In one village, hundreds of bubbles, very pink, float past like an airborne garden. I cannot see the children blowing them. Signs offer horses and "poneys," riding and boarding. A restful piece of country, even if I'm not sure where I am.

Mon Ange, my vigilant advocate, keeps checking with the bus driver about my stop in Pontorson where my B&B is located. She relays that a bus awaits this one to connect with Mont-Saint-Michel. Once we arrive, we embrace and air kiss twice like old French friends. I promise to send postcards next week when I arrive in Collioure, a Mediterranean village she's fond of. She blesses me with another thumbs-up benediction, and I leave the bus.

The next bus driver speaks little English. I show him a map with my B&B on it. He nods vigorously; I relax. The ride becomes magical when suddenly Mont-Saint-Michel looms out of the haze. Again, the thrill of disbelief: *I am really here!* We have barely left the Beauvoir bus stop, when the driver announces, "La Jacotière!" and turns to look at me. He explains very rapidly, *"ici,* here" or, chin gesture, *"la-bàs,* there." I have a choice – I think. Well, I don't want to end up out at Mont-Saint-Michel with this suitcase, so I hazard *"Ici. Merci."*

Mistake.

I check my map and guidebook. I have left the bus too early. The sign says that I am just leaving Beauvoir. The B&B is the *next* town. As it has done for 1,000 years, Mont-Saint-Michel emerges like a mirage in the distance, a vision of hope for yet one more pilgrim, this one rolling a suitcase on the highway because this country road has no shoulder or traffic or buildings, just windswept meadow, apple trees pink with bloom, and the vast horizon along the sea. Yes, Beauvoir, "beautiful to see," is aptly named. *Pas de problème.* I'll simply enjoy my journey.

I continue walking and look for the *biscuiterie* celebrated by my guidebook. Perhaps I'll find some coffee and a nibble. I do find La Biscuiterie, world famous for its shortbread cookies. Inside, I find many varieties of butter cookies, madeleines, sables, all available for sampling, but no coffee. A hearty British woman recommends the biscuits: "... seriously crumbly!" I taste. Yes, very. I make several loops around the outlet, sampling each time and find a small box of cookies. I also purchase some postcards and small book of photos of the Mont to compensate for the missing camera. My shoulders and suitcase cannot carry more.

Back on the highway, I step right along toward the Mont in the haze. Occasional cars approach. When I hear them coming, I just pull onto the grass and wait. After 24 hours of detours, I know where I'm going. Where I am doesn't matter.

La Jacotière is a stone farmhouse set in an expanse of farming fields and a sweeping view to the sea and the Mont. When I finally arrive after an hour of walking, the door is locked. A sign says, "*Complet*." Is it full with me or without me? Do I still have a reservation? I press the door bell and hear it ring far away inside. Nobody comes. *Pas de problème.* I shall simply sit in the garden with my book and biscuits until someone arrives.

An hour passes and no one appears. I walk toward the cluster of businesses at the intersection to find a water closet then a *café crème* at Brioche Dorée while I hatch Plan B. Despite the many tour busses and brisk traffic on the causeway leading to the Mont, the chain hotel across the street advertises *chambres libres* (vacancies) for 54 euros, about 70 dollars. I can stay here if I need to. First, I'll walk back to La Jacotière with this suitcase which has become part of my body. I left a note, but Claudine may be gone for the day.

I see the British couple with their wine glasses first. Claudine, very small, 50-ish, a pixie, is unloading her car.

"Ahh!" she greets me with two air kisses. "You are one people!" She has booked me into the honeymoon suite by mistake.

The British gentleman wags his finger between himself and his wife. "We are *two* people!" Much laughter and Franglais as Claudine explains that she had morning appointments and didn't know when I would arrive. *Pas de problème.* So many difficulties, inconveniences, really, dissolve into *pas de problème.* Perhaps that is one gift of a pilgrimage. ###

Chapter 10
Shell of a Pilgrim

Not I, nor anyone else, can travel that road for you.
You must travel it by yourself.
It is not far. It is within reach. – Walt Whitman

Mont-Saint-Michel has loomed large in my plans ever since I first thought about visiting France. A spiritual fortress, once cut off from the mainland by fierce tides, it has drawn pilgrims and the curious for more than 1,000 years. I, too, am inexplicably drawn to this mystical place dedicated for fifteen centuries to the sword-wielding protector Saint Michel, but not as a tourist. Rather, I seek to experience something that cannot be seen or defined, so my lost camera seems trivial. Postcards can record the architecture and scenery.

I walk a sandy path that parallels the paved causeway six feet above me where few cars travel this afternoon. Overcast sky and a breeze, cool and damp off the English Channel refresh me for the half-mile walk. A few couples and small groups pass, returning from the Mont. Is this slack tide? Or is it coming in? The ruffles of waves suggest the latter. I scan the path strewn with stones and the nearby sandbar for a shell souvenir. Then I spy and pocket a fragment of scallop shell, symbol of pilgrims for centuries, especially those hiking the *camino* to pay homage to St. James at Santiago de Compostela, Spain. Perhaps as I journey toward elder grace, I, too, am a *pèlerin,* a wanderer, a pilgrim.

So, I consider what turns ordinary travel into a pilgrimage. Must a true pilgrimage prove something? To God? To one's self? To both? Must the goal be sacred? Sacred to whom? Does effort count? I mean, does simply beginning or trying constitute a worthy goal, or must a true pilgrimage surmount deprivation, sacrifice, or a deliberate challenge? Must one finish the course? If a pilgrimage were simply a challenge, I could have met it by creating an elaborate wedding needlepoint for Trina and Steve or by teaching Susanna, a grandmother, English past first-grade level. Why does one have to *go* somewhere? The origins of the word pilgrimage give me clues: to go beyond one's own fields, one's own borders of home. One must test whether the truths we know at home are true elsewhere, for example, the kindness of strangers like Marie Ange. Perhaps one must test one's self without the support of community, for though one may travel with a band of fellow pilgrims, one must ultimately discern the stirrings of spirit alone. Such is the essence of the holy – wholeness, completeness.

If so, then I am, indeed, a pilgrim seeking Wholeness, a time apart to discern a new direction at this 62-year crossroad in my life. I must learn how to grow old with grace, confidence, and refreshed purpose. Perhaps this 1000-year old Mont can teach me about perseverance, about rising above the similarly turbulent and sometimes muddy ebb and flow of my own tides.

Now the ocean races past me, "as fast as a horse can gallop," say the locals, toward the salt meadows as I walk and ponder the more predictable life transitions. For example, we create elaborate ceremonies and class trips for students who conclude a course of study. Newlyweds slip away on honeymoons to luxuriate in time to know each other. Mothers, especially in Scandinavia, have maternity leave to settle into their new roles and learn to love the mysterious little beings they have created. Society celebrates christenings, Bar Mitzvahs, baptisms, weddings, and funerals to celebrate significant life transitions. Yet as we age, what do we do for ourselves to mark a change from one life role to the next, from full-time caregiver to family consultant, from professional person with a title to a "once-was" with time on her hands? A few, I suppose, have retirement parties as they pull back from long-held positions; however, we lifelong caregivers don't retire. Ever. Instead, I embark upon a time alone to learn the next part of my life journey. Yes, this trip is a pilgrimage to a richer, more integrated identity – because my life is sacred no matter my age.

Enough brooding. By 4:30 in the afternoon, I have reached the base of the Mont that now soars hundreds of feet above me; the site closes at 7 p.m. My guidebook advises avoiding the schlocky touristy entry, so once through the main gate, I quickly veer left and begin to climb steep, stone stairs to the rampart level, avoiding the "town" below. I watch my feet, for after a thousand years of wear, the hundreds of rock steps are uneven and hazardous. Handicap access does not exist.

About halfway up the first flight of stairs, I spot a garden tucked between stone buildings with leaded glass windows and small chimney pots. The meandering walkways lead me past hundreds of stone stairs, pocket gardens, and shade trees; past monolithic stonewalls and panoramic vistas of sea, sky, and spires. A gentleman chats companionably in French as we survey the heavy wooden sled once used to haul goods up the nearly vertical wall several hundred feet off the ground. *"C'est un mystère ... une merveille ...* It's a mystery, a marvel." We cannot imagine how people could be strong enough to live here.

That the Mont was created by human hands numbs my reason, so I gaze for a while on nature, on the sea, and mud flats under empty sky and discern specks, people walking the eastern flats. I wonder vaguely whether they will be sucked into quicksand or captured by the rapidly rising tide. The vast distance between us creates a strange detachment from humans.

Now as I stroll the abbey, my brain craves retreat, this time from vastness to tiny marvels: feathers clinging to lichen on the Guest Room windowsill 500 feet above the ocean; dainty ferns growing out of crevices in the rock walls; moss tinting the carved stone archways green. The colonnaded cloister, a tranquil garden hundreds of feet above the ocean, fulfills my requisites for contemplation: blooming cosmos, vinca, tiny daisies, and other flowers; views of sea, sky, and gulls; cooing doves and trilling songbirds; graceful marble columns and statuary. Heaven on earth. No, not quite, for Revolutionary soldiers have defaced, literally broken the faces off the *bas-relief* saints. The contrast of destruction and serenity here remind me that even life on the Mont cannot provide an escape from hate at large in the world, perhaps just a clearer glimpse of a more perfect Place.

Because it is late in the day, I sometimes have entire chambers to myself before others wander in. I linger to let chattering school groups go ahead of me, then stroll in and out of chilly chambers, often in perfect solitude. The fireplace in the Guest Room, a banquet hall, stops me in my tracks. I pace off 15 feet by 7 feet. *I could park my car in there.* Another *merveille*.

Around a corner, I suddenly find myself alone in an alcove at the feet of a sculpture of St. Michael himself, his sword in mid-swing overhead. This sword as symbol of faithful protection unsettles me, me whose weapon of choice is a Swiss Army knife the size of a lipstick. No, I don't understand weapons, but it is not his weapon that arrests my attention. I gaze at his face, delicate as a teenager's, then notice at waist level in front of me, his shoes. Soft shoes, like leather socks with a rolled cuff. Slipper socks. A flap of metal mesh over his instep is all his protection. I have never wielded a sword, but I've worn socks: no protection against stubbed toes, no arch support, no hard sole against sharp rocks. And the courage of this saint looms more real because his feet seem so vulnerable.

From the high cloister, I note that the notorious 40-foot tides have filled the mud flats. As wind ruffles my hair, I can see the farm fields beyond my B&B in Pontorson, all the way to Beauvoir in the south and the route I hiked when I exited the bus a mile too soon. Yesterday my view of the Mont inspired me to keep going. Now I'm inspired by gauging how far I've come. Look forward. Look back. Anticipate where I'm going. Reflect upon where I've been. Always keep moving and trust the journey. Such is the erratic progress of a pilgrim carrying a broken scallop shell.
###

Chapter 11
"Go Some Distance Away": Leonardo's Advice in Amboise

Every now and then, go away, have a little relaxation, for when you come back to your work, your judgment will be surer. Go some distance away ... – Leonardo da Vinci

Claudine serves a charming breakfast, complete with embroidered cloths, pretty blue and yellow ceramics and full coffeepot, brie, hard cheese, some kind of quiche with prunes on the bottom, croissants, baguette and toast. No need for lunch today. I grow edgy about leaving in time to catch my train, but Claudine with her spiked hair and high top, Burberry plaid sneakers has made this run loads of times. She zips around, pitches my luggage in her Peugeot and drives like a lightning bolt to the station, alternately babbling to me and fuming at traffic. She fusses at the *camion,* truck, slowing traffic," *Vite! Vite!* Quick! Quick!" but I arrive with time to spare. After quick *bisous,* check-to-cheek kisses, she flits away. I hoist my roller suitcase, cross the tracks, and view from the outgoing platform the sleepy station with faded purple doors.

Once aboard the bouncy train between Pontorson and Rennes, I meet an Australian couple. They tell me that they were delayed for a day by nurses demonstrating in Paris, blocking the tracks at Gare Montparnasse. Because I misread my ticket, I didn't return to Paris and avoided the long delay. Sometimes things work out.

I smell burning garlic but can't understand the announcement. Are we delayed? The car at the crossing has turned around and driven away. Now another driver leaves his car to talk to the conductor. He wears heavy boots and a red and yellow emblem on his shoulder. The announcement, "*Trois minutes!* Three minutes!" suggests I'll still be on time to "Rennie," as the Australian gent says. A blast of horn, three notes that sound like an elephant, and the train eases into motion. Soon we tilt left and the glass door, frosted with ferns, slides across the aisle. The train tilts right, and the door glides back where it belongs. As I sway with the rhythm of the coach, I see the locals already haying mid-May as we streak away from the coast. The conductor assures me that my *correspondance*, my connection, for Rennes is good – a huge relief since I must make a second connection in Le Mans to catch the train for Amboise.

This two-day leg to Amboise, a small city situated in Loire château country, was not pinned down months ago like all my other lodging. Instead, a few days ago I dared to trust the off-season and my guidebook to choose at random a destination between Mont-Saint-Michel and Carcassonne. Situated on the widest part of the Loire, offering both small hotel and château within walking distance of the station, Amboise will be perfect and reaffirms my old "you-go-girl!" spontaneity.

On the train to Le Mans, Marie-Odile sits across from me. She's on her way to Strasbourg to take an exam to advance as a yoga instructor *energétique*, part of an organization that provides Reiki, acupuncture, and other alternative medicine. She hopes to visit Paris after her exam, so she is very interested in my budget lodging there. I give her the hostel address and a spare map of Paris; she gives me butter biscuits from Bretagne, her home. Marie-Odile speaks French 90% of the time and tells me my French is "correct." When I tell her that I am a teacher, she asks if I teach French! Imagine! She needs to study, so we agree to stop visiting after about 30 minutes, but our conversation nurtures me all afternoon.

Now the conductor who punches my ticket tells me I was also supposed to validate the second ticket stapled to the first. I apologize. He graciously explains how to validate: *Poussez*, push, the left edge of my ticket into the yellow machine – very accommodating for the tourists. OK. I made a mistake, but I've learned what to do next time. I'll *poussez* in Tours.

During a 90-minute layover in Tours, a woman chewing a baguette and wearing a saggy black dress, babbles to me in rapid French about trying to find her connection. She thinks I'm French – must be the red scarf, the one the library folks gave me for my bon voyage gift. How many times now have I been asked directions while wearing it?

Since it's a pretty day for walking and I still have no idea whether my camera will catch up with me at the professor's place, I decide to buy a camera. A shop within sight of the station has some expensive models which I decline; however, the obliging proprietor directs me to a department store a few blocks away. Within 15 minutes, I find the store, the department, and a low-end Nikon, which will nonetheless compromise my wine budget. *Eh bien.* I need it and can sell it on eBay when I'm back home.

Eventually I am waited upon. The clerk writes a slip and gives me, not the camera, but directions to a pay station within the store. Once I pay, I am directed to a third station where I finally pick up the camera, pleased not only with my purchase and time to spare, but also with my French. None of these salespeople speak English. This smooth business transaction buoys my confidence and helps me to deflect my first unwanted advances.

After exiting the store in the busy downtown area near City Hall, I spy some shady park benches by a bus stop. I'll just install the memory chip here then photograph the Tours City Hall blazing with flowers before heading back to the train station.

I am totally engrossed in prying open the maddening plastic around the 2G chip, when out of the corner of my eye, I sense a husky, dark-haired man in a white shirt behind my bench glancing from side to side. In a moment, he sidles alongside me and throws his arm over the back of the bench, almost over my shoulder. And he twitches. His head and right hand jerk as though from tiny electric shocks. He does not look at me.

"Madam, êtes-vous dérangée? Are you upset, worried?" he asks.

I sense something not quite right about this guy. He has not offered the traditional *"bonjour"* greeting, but I feel safe enough among all the passersby to continue assembling my camera.

"*Non. Pas du tout.* No. Not at all."

He sits there with his arm behind me, legs crossed, and continues twitching. Waiting for a bus? Who knows? I quickly finish with the camera, pack up my things and walk away. At that, he leaves and, still twitching, walks in the opposite direction. Once he is out of sight, I reverse direction to photograph the plaza surreptitiously lest he think I'm photographing him. Now to catch my train.

From the quiet train station in Amboise, it's an easy walk to La Brêche, a cozy two-star hotel. The snug entryway and dark wood reception counter offer a drowsy security like great-grandmother's parlor. *Madame*, young and eager, carries my suitcase up the creaky, carpeted stairs. Because Leonardo retired in this town, all the rooms have framed prints of his art on the doors. Mine is young girl. Or is she an angel?

Brilliant light and birdsong seep into the bathroom through the nine-foot high doors. Water splashes in the fountain outside one of my several windows. I keep checking the toilet, thinking it's running.

Since I'll be here for two days, long enough for clothes to dry, I indulge in a leisurely shower-cum-laundry, kneading undies in suds under foot. I try to adjust the half-door, a clear plastic accordion affair, rather like a wraparound windshield, which extends only half way along the tub. Before I get the hang of it, I shoot water over the walls, over the toilet, and out the window. A magpie alights under shiny leaves outside the window to escape what she thinks is rain. The breeze wafting from my bathroom window and balcony will dry the floor in no time.

The next morning, I set out in beautiful breezy sun to explore the banks of the Loire and Château Clos-Lucé, the retirement home of Leonardo da Vinci. Other *châteaux* have been highly recommended, but why spend the money and precious time on a bus when I can amble here and view the Loire? First, I climb up, up, up (at least 170 stairs) for the *vue panoramique* of the entire city of 14,000: Terra cotta rooftops and a vista of the mighty Loire. Orange poppies, *coquelicots*, spring up everywhere like weeds. I descend and walk to the Clos-Lucé chateau built in 1418 to tour alone. I read everything, especially the framed maxims of Leonardo. On this, his brocade-canopied deathbed, he allegedly wept to God that he hadn't accomplished much during his lifetime. Good grief! Is there any hope then for the rest of us?

The extensive grounds beckon. Tall trees cast dappled light and bagpipes skirl as I fall in step with a school group of third or fourth graders. A little girl seems very upset, near tears.

"*Comment ça va?* What's the matter?"

"*Mon appareil ne marche pas.* My camera doesn't work."

"Would you like me to help you? Let me see…. Ah, yes." I don't know the words for dead batteries. "You'll need to ask your teacher." With no batteries to offer, I give her tissues for her tears.

After a rejuvenating espresso by the fountain surrounded by roses, some blooming and hundreds more almost ready, I consider Leonardo's belief in the interconnectedness of living things. He especially praised the artistry of the body, yet concluded that it was as nothing when compared with the spirit. Dear Leonardo gives me much to think about, especially considering this, my French quest for wise aging.

I leave the park and stroll downtown. Here I discover a pedestrian walkway where tiny shops are tucked inside half-timbered houses. A sign, "Saint Vincent de Paul" on the sidewalk points down a narrow, empty passage between two buildings. Thrift shop? I hesitate, then follow it to the door. As I mount the stairs, I recognize the unmistakable stale vanilla fragrance of second-hand goods. The two tiny rooms full of cast-off clothing hold no treasures.

Then I spot several plastic boxes of neatly folded bras. The black lace calls to me. After all, I had promised myself something black and lacy from France. But am I an 80? 90? 75? The cheerful young woman offers to help and finds a bra marked in both US and European sizes. Aha. I'm an 80. In French she suggests:

"Just go into this little room (menswear) and try it on. I will shut the door. There's a mirror over there ... "

Why not? So, I admire myself in the black lace bra – and the red – before I notice the picture above the mirror, a cheap print of the Virgin, hand to breast, averting her eyes. Perhaps because this is menswear? Or have I offended?

Enormously pleased with my bargain hunting, I go on my way with my 1€ bras from Amboise in a *Biscuiterie* bag.

Afternoon shopping. Lacy lingerie, admittedly second-hand. Espresso among the roses. No agendas. No busses. No rushing. I began to feel I'm playing hooky, but from what? Responsibility? I quickly shoo that thought from my mind with my equation: I've waited 40 years for this trip, accruing less than one vacation day per year. Forty years for 30 days of total relaxation. Forty years for 30 days of fresh perspective. Forty years for 30 days of reigniting my love affair with life. If this is hooky, it's enormously healthy. Leonardo would approve.

That evening, I savor my simple bread and cheese in a gazebo beside the widest stretch of the Loire and watch the passersby, some jogging, some taking snapshots and hurrying along. None pause to talk. Scooters rev and whine through the streets behind me. Toward sunset, two elderly couples stroll by talking animatedly and laughing. One of the gentlemen waves and calls to me.

"… *parfait pour le pique-nique, non?* Perfect for a picnic, no?"

"*Oui! Oui! Parfait!* Yes, yes! Perfect!" I raise my tomato in joyous salute. ###

Chapter 12
Not According to Plan

Courage mounteth with occasion. – William Shakespeare

The tangle started two days ago in Amboise, when I learned that the car rental office in Carcassonne would close at 6:30 p.m. tomorrow. My train will not arrive until 7:00 p.m., and I still have to get to the airport to pick up the vehicle. My host at La Brêche hands me his cell phone to try to arrange a late arrival. A warning light in my head should have flickered when the phone rang in Ireland.

"Oh, not a problem at **all**!" the lilting voice assured me. "Why, they'll be **waiting** for you! **Thank** you for choosing …" Unconvinced, I called the Carcassonne branch, just to make sure.

"Non. Non!" her crisp reply. "It is not possible. We close at 6:30 p.m." No apologies. No suggestions. Certainly, no comfort. Not only do I have to pay for a wasted rental day, I have lost a day at Professor Tapscott's place, and I have nowhere to stay tomorrow night. Rattled, I forget to ask whether the car rental office will be open Sunday when most French shops are closed.

I manage to track down a hotel in Carcassonne close to the train station and book it online. If the car rental office isn't open Sunday, I'll just remain another night. *Eh, bien.*

Pas de problème. I applaud my ease in adapting to these changes and note that I've now been on the road for 11 days without a twinge of homesickness.

How quickly things can change ...

At the Amboise train station, I meet Georgia from San Diego who, with her ex-military husband, is touring Italy, France, and England. She tells how she emails her granddaughter, 10, with photos and details of her trip to play "Where Am I?" The child easily deduced Venice from recent clues. Neither Georgia nor her husband speaks French, so I help them find connections once we arrive in Saint-Pierre-des-Cors. Like so many other women I meet, she admires my sense of adventure: "Good for you!" Then she adds, rather wistfully, I think, "I wonder if I could do the same. I've never travelled anywhere without my husband." Unwittingly, this stranger validates my late-life dream trip.

We part, and I embark upon an entire afternoon of train travel, seated with people who know each other, read most of the way, or discourage conversation. The 20-something young woman pulls carrot salad and ham from her backpack, so I am not the only one eating. My cheese does smell ripe, but I expect that the French are used to that.

From 10:30 a.m. to 7:30 p.m., I speak with no one except to ask for the water closet, until I meet an English-speaking student from Bonn in the Bordeaux station. He shows me how to use a French phone card. Insert and leave it in the phone while calling; don't swipe it. The card has one minute on it, long enough to recognize frosty Mme Non-Non: "But yes, the car rental office in Carcassonne is open Sunday, 9:00 a.m. to 6:00 p.m. Will that be all?"

Bordeaux shimmers in heat. No one wears black tights and scarves here as in the north. Instead sandals, manicured toes, and bare skin prevail. Overheated in sweater and wool socks, I feel frumpy and out of place. Disconnected. Definitely unattractive. I wonder whether the grim woman in the knitted woolen scarf does, too. Where could she have come from?

After a hot, two-hour layover, I begin the last leg of my journey toward Carcassonne. As the landscape becomes more arid and harsh, so, too, becomes my interior landscape. My only brushes with human communication are the conductor who asks for my ticket and miles upon miles of urban and small-town graffiti. Open farmland and healthy green, growing things, I find, help me to feel much less edgy.

No trees, however, grow near my sad Carcassonne hotel on a bleak side street lined with cement wall and ashcans. Mme Proprietress, with her bushy black ponytail, greets me briskly, and unlike my other hostesses, wants her 38€ on the spot. No problem, just not much of a welcome after a lonesome train ride and botched itinerary. The room, clean and cheap as promised, disappoints. The garish red and avocado zodiac bedspread clashes with jelly bean green woodwork, blue Provençal curtains and, inexplicably, a faded loon print on the wall. The lone window overlooks an alley where trains roar past a stone's throw away.

Perhaps the feeling of total alienation and invisibility happens to everyone who travels, casualty of inadequate conversation, food, and water; too much fatigue; or tepid hospitality. Culture shock, I'll learn, can ambush at times like these. I close the blinds, stash the ugly bedspread in the wardrobe, use the sky-blue blanket for a spread, and drink two tumblers of water. At least the sink works. Better.

Since it is already 8 p.m., but still light, I decide to grab a bite, then, trusting the superlatives of my guidebook, view the illuminated medieval ramparts against the evening sky. As I pick my way down the cobbled streets, laughing couples jostle me and shriek hilarity in Spanish cadence. Salsa music throbs from dance clubs.

Suddenly, the new culture does not excite or interest me. I am on overload. I must retreat. *I am not in danger*. I tell myself. *I am not in danger. Out. I need to get out. Now!* I push down the flutter of panic – and veer toward a grocery store. A young boy in a white apron approaches.

"May I help you find something, *madame*?" *My equilibrium...*

"Yes, please. Tomatoes." He leads me to a pyramid artfully bordered with green jalapeños.

"Anything more, *madame*?" *Conversation! Keep him talking!*

"... Yes ... er ... Do you have any diet Coke?"

"This way, please, *madame*." *I love this kid. I just love him!*
"Something else, *madame*?"

"No, thank you. A thousand thank yous. You are very kind." *And I mean it.* I smile. The boy smiles, too.

Back at the sad hotel, it takes me a moment to recognize English when I meet some Canadians carrying bikes up the stairs to my floor. We exchange pleasantries, and I use my voice again. Now my once-disappointing room feels snug and secure. I have found what Mon Cher calls a "crevice." In jammies, I prop myself in bed with my feast: a whole iceberg lettuce, tomato, tartar-control dried bread, a slice of chicken, smelly cheese, cookies, and diet Coke. Like a limey in the old British Navy starved for vitamin C, I even eat a raw potato. Soon the Canadian cyclists snore like crazy next door. I start to doze and the thundering night train seems to burst through my wardrobe. And I laugh. So much for sophisticated Saturday night entertainment in southern France. What would Georgia-from-San-Diego think of this adventuress now?

Sunday morning, I have a lot to figure out: how to get to the airport to pick up my car; how to get a refund for the lost day; how to drive a French car amidst Gallic drivers; and how to find the professor's place in the Montagne Noire. First, café and an Egg McMuffin, familiar fare from my homeland.

After a quick hike to view the ramparts of the Old City before tour busses arrive, I head back toward the sad hotel to check out before 11 a.m. On the Old Bridge, I come across eight or ten people taking turns photographing their group. I gesture. "Me. Take photo. You." They respond with much happy babbling, "*Si! Si! Si!*" and thrust three cameras at me.

"*Uno! Dos! Tres!*" I click. Then I gesture, "You. Me. Photo." I position myself in front of the fortress. Much excited nodding.

The older bald man takes my camera and commands, "*Todos!* Everyone!" Suddenly, his entire group surges into the photo with me. Click. Just as suddenly, he commands, "*Solo!* Alone!" All disperse. Click. He photographs me alone. We shake hands all around and part smiling. Refreshed by this convivial exchange, I am ripe for fresh adventure.

The shuttle to the airport and car rental won't leave for 15 minutes, but I decide to take a seat while the dark-haired driver enjoys his noon break. He rolls his own cigarettes, sips a coffee, eats some cherries, and listens to salsa music that reminds me of my Zumba class. His pleasure is palpable and infuses me with contentment.

My arrival at the car rental office coincides with an incoming flight, so I join the tail end of the queue. Mme Non-Non, very pretty in person, but just as brusque, shoves wads of forms at me to sign. Once everyone else has been helped, she softens, gives me a key, points to a dusty lot full of cars where I will locate mine. She assures me that the rental company will reimburse my hotel, but it never does.

A turquoise Citroën! By trial and error, I manage to roll down the windows and shift gears. While trying to open the car trunk, quite by accident, I roll down the roof. A convertible! Dodging potholes and weeds, I growl along in low gear though the rock-strewn alley much more suitable for military vehicles than brand new convertibles. I pause before merging onto the highway. Now the most dreaded adventure of all, navigating French traffic.

When we first plotted my trip, my usually intrepid son steered me away from a car rental. Blame the accident in Brazil when he had been sideswiped and sent spinning. With only three months of Portuguese under his belt, he couldn't explain, so the other driver convinced authorities that Tom was at fault. The incident took a year to resolve. At least he and his companion weren't hurt.

This spring, the professor has tried to alleviate Tom's anxiety. Besides, I cannot go to his remote village, 20 miles away, without wheels. I'm game. Then the professor sent his distressing directions: "… as you approach LeClerc Supermarché, there's a big traffic rotary … Go around that rotary as often as you need to get oriented!" My stomach cramps as I imagine being sucked into a centrifuge of raging Gallic drivers streaking around a circle and timid me, trapped, trying vainly to escape, until at last, I'm hurled through an exit. Pray God it's the right one. Now I see the sign for LeClerc. I swallow, grip the wheel, and approach the dreaded rotary.

Empty.

So, my guidebook was right about the sanctity of a long French Sunday lunch. *Tout le monde* is at home dining. Totally relieved, I take the wrong exit, return to downtown Carcassonne, recognize my error, loop back to the rotary, and exit toward Mazamet. Now the landmarks don't match my sheet of directions.

Pas de problème. I swing off yet another rotary to ask directions of the dark man selling produce. His speech sounds a mix of French and Spanish, but he repeatedly points me back the way I have just come. I buy some very fresh strawberries and asparagus then resume my journey. I circle the once-dreaded rotary for the third time and follow the signs to Toulouse. Now directions and landmarks agree, even though the "Norman church in the middle of the road" turns out to be the size of a garage. I expected a fortress.

Pollarded sycamores rustle over the empty boules court as I arrive in Saint-Denis, the little stone village that time forgot. Except for two other cars parked under these trees, it could still be the 17th century. None of the 450 souls who call it home seem to be around. I park in the afternoon shade near an ancient church surrounded by purple irises, then emerge, stretch, and look for "the second house on the left, blue slate" beyond the stone arch. All I see is a two-story house of gray stone with two doors. So, what constitutes a "house"? A separate building? A door? The building beyond this has a locked font gate, so I determine that the stone house with kindling-dry, unpainted shutters and second "Hobbit-like door," must be the place. The brass skeleton key fits. *Voilà!*

The house has not been occupied for six months, so I follow directions for opening it. This means entering the shuttered *rez-de-chaussé,* ground floor, in the dark. The blackness smells of long-ago wood smoke, cheese, and age, pleasant and reminiscent of a special kind of freedom. I fumble for the promised flashlight just inside the door, find the fuse box to turn on the electricity, and the valve to turn on the water. So far, the directions coincide with the location of things. I trust that I am in the right house.

Now I climb a tightly coiled spiral staircase to the main living level darkened by shutters. Once I pull back the French windows and throw open the shutters, sunlight streams into the living space, cozy in French blues and white. The sheer curtains, eager to play after a long winter, float out over the *allée*. Joy of joys, I spy an electric kettle on the miniscule counter. I need not hazard gas valves! I quickly brew tea, ease myself onto the sofa, and finger a threadbare quilt in Dresden plate design. "Tapscott" embroidered on the hem cinches it: I am in the right house for sure.

This dreamer, this competent dreamer has arrived. ###

Chapter 13
Idyll in Languedoc

"It is not on any map; true places never are."
– Herman Melville

Perhaps I've painlessly died and gone to heaven. Surely this is what it must be like, mindless joy where swallows swoop with abandon in porcelain blue skies; where red poppies and buttercups nod in a warm breeze; where narrow roads dappled with sunshine curve invitingly; where patches of green farmland stretch all the way to the snowcapped mirage of the Pyrénées; where a friend offers the hospitality of home. I am driving through a Monet landscape in this turquoise Citroën convertible, the breeze in my hair. Such is my Perfect Moment here in Languedoc, where white horses grazing among the poppies outnumber the tourists. And it all started with a daring decision to quit my job to maintain my self-respect. This I now know for a certainty: "acting independently" is neither character flaw nor liability.

After 15 minutes of driving twisting road bordered by a few homes, Cathar castle ruins, and 600-year-old monasteries, I arrive in Saissac, a small village with a sweeping, hazy vista of the Pyrénées. Below me, more castle ruins and a small *épicerie,* grocery store, cling to the mountainside. The tiny shop is empty save for Monsieur the

Proprietor who greets me and helps me to select cheese, which he then cuts to order. I ask which red wine he recommends, and he directs me to a Minervois, a local *terroir,* very inexpensive. A baguette, some apples. Done. We bid each other *au revoir,* and I savor the return drive home.

Back in the village of tiny stone houses, many with shutters as blue as the sky, I explore the neighborhood, walking each *rue* until it ends in meadow or someone's yard. In one, a man sets out tomato plants. No one else is outside, save a stone sculpture of the Virgin in faded blue mantle. A stone *lavoir-abreuvoir,* laundry sink/trough for animals, sits beside a dirt road, a humble reminder that for its first 300 years – or longer – this town managed without indoor plumbing. The main street needs no stop sign, and pavement touches the sides of buildings. Only potted plants and a solitary car on this empty thoroughfare tell me that people actually live here. I marvel at the quiet. Handwritten signs tell me that *La Poste,* post office, is open only three hours a day; the public library, one hour each, Tuesday and Thursday. Life here is deliciously slow.

Now the sun begins its afternoon visit to the professor's house, shining first on my lunch plate of bread, Comté, fresh asparagus, an apple, and coffee – French press, of course – as I perch on the foot-wide window ledge. Sheer curtains waft with the breeze as though breathing. Below, a shaggy dog, a Yorkie or Bichon Frisé, yowls. A nonchalant calico cat atop the high stonewall across the *allée* sniffs the grass growing through the lichen. My host has told me about neighbor Mary Jo. I call down to her as she slaps a rug against the stonewall and introduce myself. *"Enchanté!"* she exclaims. She tells me the dog is "Gizmo" and inquires after the professor.

"Il arrivera aujourd'hui. He returns today." She seems pleased.

Farther down the *rue,* a couple argues, I think, but as I can't tell what they say, their impassioned, melodic language simply adds to the lovely ambiance, the very Frenchness of the town and this 400-year-old house. In the kitchen nook, pots and pans dangle from a copper coronet suspended by chains from foot-square, hewn wooden beams. Beneath them, a plain wooden shelf holds blue and white dishes, glassware, and teapots. A French blue sofa separates this tiny kitchenette tiled in blue and white from the little living area.

Many books about France and things French slouch on the wooden mantle near a vase of lavender, a clock in golden case, and a wooden artist's model of the human body poised, it seems, in a jig. Coffee. Frenchness. An artist's model.

Coffee. Frenchness. An artist's model. And like the stroking that evokes the genie in a dusty lamp, stroking these random thoughts evokes Viviane.

Viviane and I met at a boarding house near Harvard Square, Cambridge, the spring I was 22, and she was "older than the hills." I was on my knees, hanging over a claw-footed tub washing my hair with the door open when she trotted up the stairs with her suitcase and bags. Before I could wrap my head in a towel, she stuck her head in the door. "Hello, my dear. I'm your new neighbor." I don't think she ever called me by my first name, only "my dear" in such a broad Boston accent, "dear" had two syllables. Before my hair was dry, she had invited me for coffee the next day after work.

"Come in! Come in, my dear! Take a pew!" and she offered me the only chair in the room while she sat on the bed. Stacked suitcases covered with an embroidered cloth supported a tray with doily, two pretty espresso cups, tiny spoons, a pink glass dish of sugar cubes, and *madeleines,* an elegant arrangement in this tired old room dating to 1861. Viviane was anything but tired. Her creased cheeks and sprinkling of brown age spots on her hands made me, in youthful ignorance, think she was 75, 80, maybe more. Surely, those perfectly even teeth were dentures. Blue eyes behind her plain gold glasses and the faded sienna in her hair made me think she must have once been a fiery redhead. Even now, she radiated youthful energy. I pulled my chair closer, as though drawing toward a warm stove.

"Now isn't this just wonderful, having coffee? I so enjoy young people and all their ideas! You must tell me everything you've been doing, my dear. Have you lived here long?"

"About 2 months."

"Do you like it here?

"Well, it does get pretty chilly at night. Sometimes I just crawl into bed and read as soon as I get home from work."

"Oh, that Charles!" Charles was the landlord. "He's a funny old stick. Always thinks he's on his way to the poor house. 'Turn down the heat! Turn off the lights!' I've known Charlie since Hector was a pup. Never the same since Evelyn died, poor man. Ah, well, don't worry about the heat, my dear. I've stayed here many times and scolded him about this before. I'll just scold him again. Now, tell me what you do all day."

So began our evening conversations. She listened intently to my boring stories about being a typist at Harvard, my confusion about returning to college, my attempts at writing poetry.

"Poetry! Oh my, but that's marvelous, my dear! Now you must keep that up. You can only become better. And keep reading, reading, reading. Which poets do you love?" When I mentioned e. e. cummings, she launched into stories about poets who had visited her home. "Oh, yes. Edward. He had a handshake like a dead fish. You can tell quite a lot about a man by his handshake. And the children wouldn't sit by Robbie Frost, my dear. They said, 'Mummy, he smells.'"

On and on went the stories. She told about being born aboard a ship during a terrific storm off the coast of Maine. "And my father, a professor of antiquities, wanted to name me Oceana. Can you imagine? Well, my dear, my mother wouldn't hear of it! And being a clever woman, she said, 'we'll name her after your great-grandmother.' And that's why I'm a Viviane. And how did you get your pretty name, my dear?" And though her name-dropping stories seemed improbable – a bit of dementia or delusions of grandeur, perhaps? – she seemed harmless, sincere, and fascinating to me, a budding romantic.

As we grew to trust each other, I told her about my microscopic love life: infatuated at 21, washed up at 22. "And now all my friends are getting married. I'm hopeless," I whined. Viviane never tried to placate me. Instead, she sympathized and shared that she, too, had once been infatuated.

"I worshipped the soles of his feet, my dear. Émile was an artist, a sculptor. A brilliant, passionate Frenchman. Oh, how I loved him!" Her eyes took on a gleam I hadn't seen before as she stared at her closet door.

"But artists are so temperamental, so terribly temperamental. Too often, he thought his work was no good, even though Pascal had offered to show it in his gallery. Some nights Émile drank too much. Yes. He always favored *pastis* ... I'd leave him working well past midnight, and when I'd come back in the morning, I'd find his sculpture smashed to pieces. Oh, my dear, it was terrible: a head over here and feet over there and dust and chips everywhere. And I'd clean it up. And he'd repent. Then, a few months later, he'd drink and smash his work again. After a while, I knew I couldn't live like this. That's when I left him to dance with Isadora ..."

"Isadora Duncan?"

"Yes, my dear, in Vienna." Was she telling the truth? I'll never know, but I chose to believe her.

After her dancing years, Viviane had returned to America then worked as a visiting nurse in Harlem and insisted, "No dear, I was never afraid." Now, with her adult children in Connecticut and France, she spends her mornings reading at the Athenaeum in Boston and afternoons writing long letters in her spidery hand and painting botanicals in watercolors. And many evenings, I took a pew.

As summer progressed, I began to make plans to return to college after a two-year hiatus. To convince myself that I could once again endure the rigors of academia, I enrolled in a poetry course at Harvard Summer School. The week before the final exam, I worried so about failing, I broke out in a rash and felt nauseous. At about the same time, the friendly Welsh boarder with the waist-length blonde braid who waitressed until she had cash for the next adventure, announced that she would be leaving soon to go pony trekking in the Rocky Mountains. Did I want to go along? A chance to travel! I could ditch the poetry exam and returning to college. What to do?

"Take a pew, my dear. Take a pew. Now, what's all this about? What are your choices?"

I explained as best I could. Viviane asked for a little clarification, but did not make any suggestions. I heard myself saying that I could put off the decision a little longer, until after my exam. If I failed, I could go trekking. Or I could return to school. Nothing had to be decided immediately.

Viviane listened, then spoke with quiet authority. "You have all the information you need to make the right decision. Know that you *will* make the right decision. Now, shall we have coffee?"

The day I left for college, buoyed by my A in the poetry class, I kissed Viviane's wrinkled cheek, soft as a peony. She gave me a packet of shortbread cookies and her geranium, Emmeline. All of her geraniums had names.

After I graduated and moved to the Rockies, we corresponded for maybe 15 years until her Christmas card came back stamped "deceased." Yet now, 40 years after I met her, I discover that Viviane has been traveling all these years in the steerage of my mind. "Know that you will make the right decision," she reminds me. And most of the time, I do.

The golden clock on the mantel reads 1:30 p.m. I walk a short distance to *La Poste*, but my camera still has not arrived. *Eh, bien.* Perhaps tomorrow. In the meantime, I have my new camera. My host arrives shortly after I return. He bustles about settling in then we toast each other with the Minervois.

"Tell me about your trip," he invites, and I regale him through two glasses of wine.

"Now you tell me about that painting over the mantel." I point to the canvas of a woodland pond and a smiling pig leaping gracefully off a dock into it.

"Oh, that." He chuckles. "A friend gave it to me for a milestone birthday. He said it represents 'confidence at mid-life.'"

I laugh so hard I nearly blow Minervois out my nose.

My host regards me with bewilderment and sips his wine. ###

Chapter 14
Opening Doors

Seek and ye shall find ... – Matthew 7:7

The train slides into the station in the soft pink wash of *crépuscule*, French twilight. After 11 hours of travel and three transfers, each to a smaller line, I have arrived at my destination, Collioure, where the Pyrénées tumble into the Mediterranean, and if my guidebook is to be believed, where few tourists flock. Certainly, no one is hanging around the small red brick station or riding this milk run route with me.

I lurch toward the vestibule between cars, trundling my suitcase, and wait for the doors to open. Nothing. Of course. On this older, nearly obsolete car, nothing will be automatic. I look for a button, a lever, a bar. Nothing. Ah. Finely printed instructions tell me *poussez*, push down, against the chrome handle. I *poussez* with all my weight. Nothing. Now adrenaline begins to fizz in my chest. I'm trapped. Alone. No passengers in the cars on either side of me. I beat down swelling panic. *I can do this. I can do this. I CAN DO THIS!* The French trains are hideously efficient. I have mere moments to escape or wind up in Spain for the night. I lunge like a buffalo in rut against the chrome bar and ever so slowly the door glides to the right. At precisely that moment, the conductor blasts three shrill notes on her whistle. Go. Now. I hunch my shoulder bag, grab my suitcase, and graze the step as I leap to the pavement. My suitcase bounces once. The train vanishes.

I find myself alone in a deserted station where poppies grow through cracks in the pavement. *Eh, bien. Pas de problème.* I have escaped calamity, I have a phone number for a taxi, and a reservation for a room on the edge of the sea. Surely, I can walk there if the taxi does not come.

As I walk toward the car park away from the rails, a mild evening breeze rustles the sycamores surrounding the *cul-de-sac*. I find the telephone box, wrangle the door open, and phone the taxi. In my most deliberate French, I make my wishes known. Then I wait. Several cars, usually full of teens, loop around the *cul-de-sac* and speed off. A burly fellow roars up on a motorcycle, then kills the engine and parks it in small shed. He ignores me. I don't feel threatened. Perhaps it's the residential neighborhood and all the trees or my dreamy haze, for at the age of 62 I have finally glimpsed the Mediterranean, the sea of my calendars and my imagination.

About 15 minutes later, the taxi pulls up. Monsieur le driver hops out, greets me in French, and stashes my bags. "You are English?"

"*Non, je suis Américaine.*"

"Ah …" Side by side, chatting in French, we ride companionably through the narrow, leafy streets, a jumble of two- and three-story, terra cotta tiled houses adorned with wrought iron balconies and flowers. Trees lend grace to this fascinating place. We emerge at last by the teal green expanse of the Mediterranean, gilded in sunset. I gasp. My driver smiles and nods.

"Yes, yes. It is God's country, no?" Yes. God's country. Heavenly scenery and enough serenity to enjoy it. I smile remembering the taxi-bus driver in Reykjavik claiming exactly the same connection, God's country – just as I used to boast in Wyoming. God's country. I like the humility of this man.

The taxi has skirted the bay and now winds along a narrow highway that climbs to the top of a promontory, the tail end of the Pyrénées, where my hotel clings to the cliffs at the southern edge of the bay. He adroitly turns the taxi in a small parking space perched above the trees and above the roof of my hotel, then apologizes that he cannot drive closer to the entrance. I gladly pay $12 for the ride which spared me at least a mile and half of walking.

Now I pause on the stair: I am really here. The Mediterranean surges below me, street lamps gleam on the opposite side of the bay beneath the crenelated silhouette of what appears to be a castle. A breeze, perhaps from Tunisia, gently lifts my hair and teases the fringe on my scarf. Jasmine scented chill reminds me that it's time to find my room.

I heft my suitcase down two flights of stairs to a small patio outside a glass door. I punch in the code and pull. Nothing. Try again. After nine or ten attempts, I buzz the intercom though I know that no one is on duty at this hour. Already my mind flits to Plan B: sleep on this terrace and relieve myself discreetly in the jasmine. After all, no one else seems to be here. I punch the code one last time and slump against the door – which glides open. Aha, it was a *poussez*, a pusher, not a *tirez*, a puller. Doors. I am still learning to open them.

This door enters directly into a dining room, an eyrie of arches and glass. The glass tables and lucite tops of the chairs disappear into the vista; I feel I am floating above the sea, the town, the cliffs. In the reception alcove, I see a rack of keys. Mine, for *chambre* 20, is attached to a nickel fob the size of a doorknob, impossible to lose. A letter addressed to Madame Schilling welcomes me and explains the breakfast hour. Now to find the room. None of the rooms in reception have numbers.

I cross the dining room and go out the far glass door, hoping the same code works for all of these doors.   A walkway edged by low balustrade clings to the side of the building where numbers mark two sets of arched, weathered, wooden doors, like shutters. I count 21 … 20. My room? My key opens the ancient lock. I pull the barn doors wide, secure each with wrought iron clasps in the stucco wall and face two more doors, actually French windows, which easily push inward. So, this is a *lavabo,* a bare-bones room with bed and sink, no toilet or shower. When I booked it, I figured that 77 bucks would land me only a room on the back, never an ocean view. Yet here I sit on my comfy bed, out of most of the breeze, looking past my toes through double doors that open onto a wind-twisted pine and the dusky expanse of the sea. I gaze until sky and sea merge in the darkness. I pull shut the barn doors, secure the metal hasps at top and bottom, push the French doors until they click, then burrow under the covers, literally locked into my *chambre*.

Opening and closing doors. At 62, this has become a metaphor of my life. So many doors close now as I age: fertility, career, being needed. Other doors open: grandchildren, travel, independence. Sometimes I see exactly where I want to go, but cannot get there. Sometimes the doors are unmarked; I must trust my inner wisdom. Sometimes I have a key; sometimes not. When to push? When to pull? I must try to learn different combinations of turning, twisting – trusting. Doors, I find, stay closed or screech on rusted hinges, not because they're old, but because they aren't used. I have more to learn from French doors. ###

Chapter 15
Dreamy Days in Collioure

If a man could pass through Paradise in a dream,
And have a flower presented to him as a pledge that he had
really been there,
And if he found that flower in his hand when he awoke, –
Aye, what then?
– Samuel Taylor Coleridge

Dozens of sailboats glide along the Mediterranean horizon. Windsurfers as intrepid as Icarus fly along open sea beyond the breakwater. Little sailors like this child maneuvering his dinghy no bigger than a bathtub with crib sheet sail, stay in the bay. He pops along like a cork, tacking the lively waters. Another perfect day of dazzling sun, breezes, and dusky teal and cobalt sea flecked with white caps.

Such is the Saturday scene as I stroll to Café Sola for my morning coffee and Wi-Fi amid a babble of languages, the rumble of traffic. The six-story stone *château*, looms over the bay as it has for 600 years. After about an hour of email, brass music suddenly blares from the beach. I pack up and hurry outside to follow the festive sound.

I find a brass band, all right, but not like any I've seen. About 20 musicians dressed in hilarious silver *lamé* and funky hot pink outfits, strut and play "Joshua Fit the Battle of Jericho," crazy-funny like Mardi Gras. A 50-something guy, balding with silver tinsel Mohawk, sways and oompahs with a hot pink tuba marked amblingband.co.uk. Hot pink marabou feathers adorn other trumpet and trombone bells. Another guy jives in pink patent platform shoes and slinky silver jumpsuit with long ruffles on sleeves. A saxophonist in a silver wig gyrates with her sax, the spring-loaded stars on her headband bouncing in time. But the loony outfits can't disguise the talent of these extroverts. They're good – and their *joie de vivre* reverberates off the gray walls of the château and pastel stone houses that cascade toward the bay like stairs.

Another group, far enough away not to compete for sound space, sports equally ludicrous outfits with a piggy theme. One trim, attractive woman in Mad Hatter chapeau with springs and other oddities waving atop it, wears funnels topped with fabric piggy snouts dangling carrot tops over her breasts. Extreme? Oh, yes. The drummer looks like an Elvis crossed with Miss Piggy. Glued on sideburns, star-shaped shades, and 6 o'clock shadow. And all of them look like they are having the time of their lives, especially the woman rocking with her trumpet in her wheelchair.

Sometimes the glitzy bands combine for a reprise with bands dressed more conservatively in black t-shirts printed with the band name or starkly white cotton. None of the groups beg for money. A local tells me it's all for exhibition. Just for fun.

Later that afternoon, the bells of Our Lady of the Angels peal wildly. From this patio across the bay, I see a slow procession heading toward the church, past sunbathers and swimmers. A funeral? A wedding? Yet another life event will be celebrated within the sheltering walls of Our Lady. How many weddings has it now seen? Thousands? Oh, if those stones could speak ...

Tonight, the air is hot and still. I consider a swim, but have not yet figured out how to lock everything in my room and manage the key with the heavy knob. Now the jasmine scented breeze picks up, carrying the wild, impassioned drum solo of "Star Wars" across the bay. I picnic on the patio, translate the newspaper for a while, then suffused in the happiness of the day, I sleep.

The next morning while I have coffee at Les Délices Catalanes, a tall man walks by with two bouquets of orange roses. Ah, yes! Fête des Mamans, Mother's Day. Already people fill the sidewalks, many carrying baskets with their purchases from the Farmers' Market. Cherries must be a good buy today. Apricots and radishes, too. I'll visit the market before I join the locals for Mass at Our Lady. I wonder whether this sacred space retain The Good, too?

Outside the entrance of the church, a bearded man sits on the ground, hopeful hat on his knee. Because the church has only a few tiny windows, way up high, I plunge into gloom when I descend the stairs, leaving behind the sun-soaked Mediterranean morning. Only the six children dressed in white and another six dressed in what looked like white habits and albs brightened the darkness. Today they appear to celebrate First Holy Communion. The priest fusses over everyone, lining them up, tilting the candles they carry just so. All the families are taking photos, so I easily slip into the crowd. Then the procession begins as the youth carry their flickering candles, simple symbols of hope into the dusky, ancient building.

The First Communicants and another six light their candles off the Paschal candle. At the end of the service, after several more lovely songs about children and The Way, the youngsters pose in front of the 40-foot tall, gilded Baroque altarpiece for photo ops. Again, I join the families and take photos, too – souvenirs of innocence and hope.

Yet I wonder about these children. Are those wearing habits already headed for a religious life? At 14-16 years old? And what of the others? Where will their faith journeys take them? Did the beggar at the door make his first communion here? For today, at least, these youngsters grasping candles have the full support of their faith communities and families. All of our children need candles in the dark.

Once outside the church, I blink to adjust to the sun dazzle. Drifts of white paper hearts and red rose petals in the gutters tell me that yesterday's procession was, indeed, a wedding. I scoop a handful and tuck them in my purse. Back home, these petals will prove that I was really here, that Collioure was not a dream.

Now the jazz ensemble in the shade eases into a languid rhythm. Another dreamy day in Collioure. I fall into step with a grandpa with tattooed biceps, pushing a baby carriage and lapping an ice cream cone. No one rushes here. People walk, talk, and eat together. They don't isolate themselves in autos or with cell phones and *ordinateurs*, laptops. Life seems more connected here, even to this outsider who finds it peculiar that it's forbidden to walk on the grass, but fine to bare your bosom on the beach. Despite these strange customs, I don't feel lonely here, even now, three weeks away from home. If I stay longer, will I feel homesick?

At Maison Anaik Noblet, where diners enter a VW van to order, "Unchained Melody" throbs, and I think of the Mon Cher look-alike in the church this morning. He had shorter hair, cut to the neck of his olive drab t-shirt, but the same high cheekbones, coloring, and build. Longing rises in my chest, and I decide not to wait but to buy his fisherman's sweater today, the *classique* style, off-white with deep blue stripes. OK, so the 20-euro price tag blows my daily budget, but he's worth it, I tell myself. I can skip the glass-bottomed boat cruise. For I need no more marvels in this place of so many Perfect Moments. This weekend each of my senses has found delight many times over. Music, music, and more music. Strawberries from Spain. Sunlight on my hair and shoulders. Jasmine-scented breezes. And always the white sails, free as gulls, against a blue horizon. This is the way life should be: sunny, friendly, beautiful, and slow enough to savor it all.

When I began this journey, my kids worried that I'd find my heart's desire and never come home. Maybe they're right to worry. Two days aren't nearly enough here in Collioure. I want to stay forever. ###

Chapter 16
Derailed in Collioure

Truly, nothing is to be expected but the unexpected.
– Alice James

When I arrived here in Collioure, enchanted with my cliff-dweller room perched over the Mediterranean, I never wanted to leave. Thanks to today's rail strike, *la grève*, I won't. I could do worse than be stranded on the edge of the Mediterranean.

I had risen at 6 a.m. to have time to pack and then walk about a mile to the train station to save cab fare. When I arrive, the station is eerily quiet. The man who had stashed his motorcycle here the night I arrived plays with his Golden Retriever and tells me about *la grève.* Hadn't my guidebook warned about these unpredictable train strikes? He points to a tiny, handwritten sign on the station door. Sure enough. No trains. Can I still travel to Arles today? This is a tiny stop at the best of times, hardly a station with many daily connections, much less direct ones. The burly man, whose Golden knows more French than I do, suggests that I take the bus to Perpignan, perhaps make connections, *correspondances* there?

"Where can I catch the bus?"

"Ici. Here."

"OK."

An enterprising scruffy, older guy dropping off his daughter, who speaks more Spanish than French and no English at all, offers to drive me to – somewhere – for 150 euros. I decline, of course. At about the same time, a young woman leaps out of a red car, utters breathless goodbyes, and dashes to the station as her friend speeds away. I explain *la grève* as she tugs at the locked station door. We share our frustrations, but she seems in good spirits, despite her botched departure. Sara, 22, with huge eyes and ingénue face chirps, "*D'accord!* OK!" to almost everything I say. She suggests that we walk back into town to catch the bus to Perpignan, a much larger city. Both of us, she claims, can make connections there. After waiting at the stop for 15 minutes, a bus arrives, but it cannot take us where we want to go. *Eh bien.*

Sara chirrups, "Let's have a coffee!" Brilliant. We stroll toward the many outdoor cafes on the beach and become the first customers on Café Copacabana's outdoor terrace where morning sun glitters on the sea. I place my French-English dictionary on the table between us, and referring to it now and then, we converse companionably for the next two hours.

Sara is visiting friends in Collioure but en route to Perpignan about 20 miles north of here to take exams in logistics. Her home is in Champagne in the north. "That's why I'm not tanned like the locals," she jokes. She has never been to the U.S., but seems very curious in a delightfully innocent way. "What do you eat for breakfast? Sweet or salty?"

We talk about the creepy guy at the station, about her love life – no one yet. I point to the two dozen navy commandoes in sleek wetsuits in the nearby surf and suggest she pick one. She laughs. I ask how to say frogmen in French; same as English. How about "snorkel" in French? Turns out it's "tuba." I try to explain why I'm laughing at the image of frogmen with tubas and resort to drawing a cartoon on a napkin. She gets it and laughs, too.

Just as she has with the bus driver and the waiter, Sara offers to do the talking to re-book my hotel for at least tonight. I thank her but insist that it's important for older women to be independent. She smiles, agrees, hands me her phone, and lets me bumble through my conversation. All is well.

Within two hours, Sara has coordinated a ride with a friend. I have booked myself back into Hôtel Les Caranques, canceled my hotel in Arles for tonight and maybe tomorrow, depending on the length of *la grève*. I'm flexible until Sunday at 4 p.m. when I'm booked on the ferry from Nice to Corsica. As we prepare to part, Sara and I exchange addresses, and I urge her to visit me if she comes to the States. She gives me the sweetest hug goodbye with the customary two kisses. Now Collioure, so postcard pretty feels friendly, too.

Late afternoon, I walk to the downtown phone booth for the third time to call the French National Railway Company SNCF "traffic line." The recording is too fast to grasp, but I think the strike continues until 8 a.m. tomorrow. Later concierge Rosie, German-born and here 29 years, tells me she couldn't understand the message, either, except that the strike does end at 8 a.m. tomorrow. My train would have left at 7:47 a.m.

I continue to Café Sola to alert friends and family to my change of plans and find an email from my daughter:

Mama,

I'm so excited that you were able to drive a convertible! That's awesome!! We received your postcard. Merci!

I visited Mon Cher today. He had called me after his trip to the hospital – typical man! – but he's OK so please don't worry. He made it sound like he was deformed, but it's truly not bad, just a couple of stitches where he fell on his head while fishing. NO WORRIES!! He tells me that he's leaving June 2 because his dog sitters are going elsewhere. I'm sure he'll inform you. So, Steve and I will bring him to the bus stop and check on Kitty until you get home …

Very carefully, I set my espresso cup on its saucer and slip into Lamaze breathing. He's leaving. A week before I return. And he didn't even tell me. In fact, he hasn't emailed for two days. Maybe he stayed off-line or went fishing, and I make excuses. Again.

I say it again to try to believe it: Mon Cher is leaving and won't be there when I return. When will I see him again? *Will* I see him again? The last time he abruptly changed plans, he had wanted to move to New Hampshire to be close to me. I had funneled his resume to my department head, and he'd been hired for a couple of courses.

Togetherness was within grasp after months of long-distance getting-to-know-you calls and letters. He looked for housing via the Internet. Then three weeks before the start of semester, he suddenly moved to the Virgin Islands to teach there. My department head had to tell me – he didn't – and I didn't see him again for eight months. Sure, he phoned every morning for a few minutes and made leisurely weekend calls from St. Thomas. Those made me feel special, but it wasn't the same as touching or doing things together. His sweet letter full of bougainvillea petals nourished my romantic notions, but not my longing for companionate love. Now I must confront the very raw possibility that his commitment to our togetherness is a mirage, a convincing, enticing illusion always and forever just beyond my grasp. It hurts.

When I was a little girl, about 3 or 4 years old, my older cousin brought me to the sandlot playground to try the slide. Halfway up the steep stairs of this silver mountain, I lost courage, but she urged me on, warning, "Don't look down." On top, I clung to the edges, paralyzed with anxiety. Kids queuing up pressured me to take my turn. I let go and slid – smack – onto my bottom on the stony ground. No one had taught me to land on my feet.

Well, I cried all the way home, hurt and humiliated. My Auntie Helen held me and rocked me, and to make me stop crying, slipped onto my finger a little gold ring with a heart-shaped, red glass gem. "If you cry on your ring, your tears will melt the stone," she cajoled. I grasped her more tightly with my left arm, buried my face and tears into her neck –

and held my right hand and ring away from my face. As a tiny girl, I knew to protect my heart from melting, but now?

My espresso has gone cold. And bitter. I walk back to my hotel as in a trance, not seeing Collioure's many charms. This evening, my inner landscape demands my attention more than the pale Mediterranean shimmering beyond my open French doors. Chilled, but not from evening breeze, I gaze numbly at the subdued sunset and deepening colors of the sea. ###

Chapter 17
La Tramontane: Winds of Change

Le vent qui vient à travers la montagne me rendra fou ...
The wind coming over the mountain will drive me mad ...
– Victor Hugo

The next morning, wind torments the pine tree and rattles two sets of shuttered doors. I've closed them to this gale that roars like tractor-trailer trucks and nearly blows a patio table into the sea. Even so, the lunatic wind seeps into my room and rustles wooden coat hangers on my clothes rack. Whitecaps frost the sea, hundreds of them rearing and plunging toward these cliffs.

On this deceiving, sunny morning, I hesitate before venturing out. In Wyoming, fierce wind like this frightened me. It could gust without warning, once tumbling my neighbor's shed down the alley like a cardboard box, often overturning semis on the Interstate highway, or crashing cottonwood limbs to the ground. A breeze may feel like soft human breath, but raging wind is soulless, remorseless, and cruel. Where else have I braced myself against invisible force?

A few weeks after Mon Cher abruptly changed plans and moved to the Caribbean instead of closer to me, I gave myself a cruise to Star Island, a rocky outcropping nine miles off the coast of New Hampshire. Several times each summer, I'd treat myself to the tranquility of blue horizon, open sky, and a few hours on the windswept island once inhabited only by fishermen. However, on this September trip, the very last of the season, the small ship rolled and plunged through heavy seas. Waves broke against the hull, splashing all the way to the third deck. The cold stung my face like a thousand ice picks, and despite a woolen jacket and hat, I felt no warmth. If I had been thinking rationally, I would have left the top deck for hot coffee in the salon. Instead, I clung to the third deck rail to endure the sting of icy wind that distracted me from the worse sting of abandonment. I rage at Mon Cher who claims he loves me "dearly," yet who has repeatedly demonstrated that he's unreliable. I rage at myself for tolerating a fantasy, for thinking it better than nothing at all. I cannot control the tearing wind, only hide from it. However, much in my life I can control: Mon Cher is in my life because I asked him in. I can withdraw the invitation. I can refuse to be convenient like Pepto Bismol in the fridge.

Enough. I will not stay inside *ma chambre* and brood. Instead, bowed against the wind, I stagger toward Café Sola for my morning email. In this sunny hurricane, the French commandos from Fort Miradou CNEC, a navigation school, two to a Zodiac, paddle futilely, bobbing and spinning like toys. They drill in the Ravin du Douy boat launch area, deflating their Zodiacs, packing up, jumping into the water with laughs and gusto, then re-inflating, launching, and returning. I count two groups of 24 men, totally camouflaged by their clothing, life jackets, and face paint. Other times, fully dressed in camouflage and black boots, they jump off the *quai* frontwards, backwards, pirouetting, a few moments of levity in what appears to be arduous training.

At the café, a French TV weather forecast murmurs under the hum of conversation. My espresso warms and wakens me to full alertness. Today the waiter mingles with customers, so I ask if this relentless wind is Le Mistral.

"Non." He explains that Le Mistral is nomenclature of Provence. This, he tells me, is La Tramontane, a wind from the north funneled between the Pyrénées and Massif Central. *"Eh, bien,"* he says. "Tomorrow will be fine."

Fortified by a second coffee and two hours of mail and journaling, I'm still not ready to respond to Mon Cher's oh-by-the-way email announcing his intention to leave my apartment and cat early. I am, however, ready to explore the back streets of Collioure, now strangely quiet for Le Tramontane has blown the locals and tourists inside. The gelato sellers and their carts have disappeared from the rue de Vauban. Now the gilded carousel on the *quai* sits silent, the dirt *terrain de boules,* the boules court, empty. Even the wise gulls won't brave this screaming wind.

In a shop on the rue Rière an espadrille maker carves a sole at his bench, backed by bolts of blue, green, red, and awning striped canvas. Shop windows of ceramics in molten yellow, terra cotta, and cobalt splashed with Mediterranean designs draw me inside to browse. Colors energize. Thoughts of Mon Cher intrude. I push them away, cover them with images from the shop. The shopkeepers gladly talk as trade is slow. They are used to La Tremontane but come to work, anyway.

Up the steep, narrow streets I wander past sherbet-hued buildings, pink, mauve, yellow, with elaborately carved wrought iron bars protecting ground floor windows. What's behind the narrow doors dainty with lace curtains and crusty with magenta paint? A profusion of geraniums cascades from wrought iron balconies. I turn a random corner and a floppy pink sunhat entices me into a tiny boutique. The door chimes tinkle.

Madame and I exchange "*bonjour.*" I know my etiquette.

"The hat is very pretty."

"Ah, yes. But today it blows away. You will need a scarf also!" I finger several scarves as pricey as the hat, and assure her I will think about this. While I buy postcards, we chat about our children; both of us have four. We say our good byes. Further along this new *rue*, a small cheerful painting of a red poppy catches my eye. Though the shop bell tinkles, I cannot see the shopkeeper so I call out, "*Bonjour, madame,*" as I walk toward the rear of the shop.

A baritone returns my *bonjour*. I can tell he is grinning, even before I apologize. "Hey, no problem. I get called *madame* all the time." Thus, I meet Howard from New York, an ex-pat for 13 years. As I peruse starkly beautiful floral paintings and jewelry carved from red agates, he tells me that his French wife is the artist, and he is the artisan who makes bracelets. He explains how he migrated from New York, beginning with vacations that became longer and longer. Having a native wife eased his relocation considerably. When I comment on the weather, he describes the freak snowstorm last winter that iced the cobbles and forced locals to stay indoors. For nearly half an hour, the colorful inventory and conversation relieve me from thoughts of Mon Cher.

Now, head bent low, buffeted by the wind, I hike the hill to my hotel, retreating to the stability of my *chambre* and my bed. I will try for a while, at least, to shake out this wrinkled relationship that I seem determined to hang onto like a favorite but threadbare garment. Dusky lavender storm cloud scuttles along the northern horizon while the sun descends in the west and the sea heaves five-foot swells gray-green like old Coca-Cola bottles. Across the bay above the hurricane wind, the bells of Our Lady of the Angels toll from the tower that once served as a lighthouse, a beacon for those in peril at sea. Centuries of raging Tramontane have barely touched this venerable church. The aged building remains strong, vital, and relevant from light and youth within. Indeed, the scouring wind has only smoothed the roughness of the stone. Perhaps I can learn from this.

Before I shutter my hotel door, I watch the commandoes from my balustrade. Their launch, like a lobster boat with a high stern, thunders off, smacking swells, barreling over the heaving sea. Oh, dear God! Man overboard! Then another man. And another. Aha! Just one more exercise, this jumping off a speeding boat into four- and five-foot swells. I haven't jumped overboard voluntarily, but have, nonetheless, plunged into my own churning sea. Do like the commandoes do: Swim. Swim upwards. Swim toward the light.

Tomorrow will be fine, said my waiter. Storms, both inner and outer, will pass. Wind simply plays its part in a natural cycle to blow away stagnation and debris, to blow away my fantasies. Mon Cher has enhanced my life, of course, but I do not need a fantasy to have a fascinating life. My rage begins to ease, even as the wind grabs my wooden doors and tries to wrench them from my hands. I grip the aged handles, jerk the doors shut, and lock myself into *ma chambre.*

As I nibble some dark chocolate, I consider how the placid donkeys tethered on the hillside by Café Sola graze just as they have all week, and take a hint from these forbearing creatures who cannot escape the wind: Turn my back to it. Let it pass. ###

Chapter 18
Little Limpet, Big Sea

A good traveler has no fixed plans
and is not intent on arriving. – Lao Tzu

It's official: I'm tired of moving and being alone. Rain, even over the Mediterranean, has lost its charm. Today, I crave companionship and will splurge on the $14 hotel breakfast to find it. Within minutes, amid the clatter of cutlery and the aroma of warm croissants, I enjoy lively conversation with hearty and 60-ish Cathy and Chris from Sydney. He has a droll sense of humor describing "hitting cliffs" on the narrow roads to Spain. When was the last time I laughed out loud like this? The conversation and ample meal with plenty of coffee nurture me. I knew what I needed, and I found it, plus a wrap-around view of the bay. As my jolly friends and I part, we speculate whether the weather will clear. No matter. They are enjoying a trip around the world for their wedding anniversary, clearly delighting in each other's company, clearly still in love.

I have convinced myself to stay here until I return to Paris. No doubt the train strike and Mon Cher's fickleness make me seek attachment. Just as a floating limpet finds security on a *barque* keel, I find security in my *chambre* in Collioure. Here I will stay. For now, at least, I no longer crave the unknown. Sure, I'll lose a few euros because I paid deposits for the ferry to Corsica and monastery lodging in advance, but if I have what I want, how can I have lost anything? Besides, wasn't my goal at the monastery to write? I can do it here with a much better view of the sea.

So. I have done it. I've canceled my reservations in Arles, Nice, and Corsica to stay an extra week in Collioure. After walking to the train station where I snag the last seat to Paris next Saturday, I spend a couple of hours at Café Sola with prosciutto tapas and sangria while catching up on correspondence. The sun bursts out while I am online. The wind has shifted, now blowing out of Africa, and, just as the waiter predicted yesterday, today's sea calms again to the delicious cerulean blue I've seen nowhere else. Walking back from café, I see octopus, lobster and maybe 100 silvery fish in the shallows and smell seaweed. A breeze plays with my hair and pinches whitecaps out of the waves – a perfect day. Sailboats glide along the horizon. Later, when I descend the flagstone steps to the terrace with *chaises longues* and umbrellas, gulls wheel overhead without screeching. Perhaps the gull that squawked at me earlier was annoyed that a lizard disappeared before he could snap him up. I lose myself in reading *The Elegance of the Hedgehog*.

A couple I haven't yet met converses in English beneath my balustrade. I introduce myself, and Mulan responds cordially, introducing her husband, Jon, and inviting me to join them for coffee. Mulan shares a wedge of chocolate *gâteau* with both creamy and crispy layers. I contribute my packaged cookies, as well, for our spontaneous afternoon tea. My new friends are from Edinburgh, and today is their last day after a week in the area. They tell me that I missed some drama last night when late-arriving guests pounded on the door and demanded to be let in around 12:30 a.m. because they didn't have the code. Also, the gulls made a racket. Thanks to my double sets of doors, I missed it.

As travelers do, we talk about our journeys. Mulan, like so many other women, compliments my bold, solitary travel with the validation I've come to expect from other women: "Good for you!" She grew up in Amsterdam, the daughter of Chinese parents, her father a stoker on a British ship. Both she and Jon are well traveled and well educated, but I never discern their occupations. Instead, we talk about local geography and their hike to the windmill above the town.

Neither Jon nor I can exactly describe the color of the sea beneath us. He suggests, "Kingfisher? No, more greeny than bluey." I laugh, then tell them how I've missed stimulating conversation, working as I do with struggling students, who do not enjoy word play. They praise my efforts and Jon encourages me to read William Trevor, a favorite Irish writer of his.

Jon and Mulan tell me I missed a treat earlier in the week and describe the Catalan dancing Monday night: arms high, hands clasped, footwork slow and stately to brass instrumentation. Both said they nearly wept. Jon seems very curious about both Boston and the Unitarian Universalist Church and listens attentively to my perceptions.

Now we are distracted by what appears to be a wedding on the beach by Notre Dame des Anges. A woman wearing a white dress and a man in tuxedo top, white cotton drawstring pants, and white high top sneakers, stand close together by the water. A dozen or so onlookers, also in white, stand in a semi-circle facing the couple and the sea. We compliment their wedding venue and wish them a happy life. Too soon, Mulan, Jon, and I exchange e-mail addresses and wish each other farewell. For one hour, at least, this solitary traveler has been nurtured.

Later that evening, I eat *le pique-nique* on the balustrade until the rising wind drives me inside. I prefer these solitary suppers to any dining adventures in town. Right now, it's too isolating to listen to the steady murmur of the conversation, too hard to watch all the hand-holding couples. My thoughts stray to Mon Cher. We used to hold hands, too.

When I was very small, about five years old, I rode my first seesaw with an older cousin. When she hopped off, I, not knowing how to brace my knees, clunked to the ground and hurt my bottom. So it is with my maddening Mon Cher. I am still learning the fine art of our relationship seesaw. Just when we seem to be enjoying a companionable rhythm, off he hops when I least expect it, and my ego smacks the ground. I am learning to brace for these bumps. But why endure them at all? Whenever I choose, I can walk away and not play anymore.

Perhaps this sense of control and well-being inspires me to take a photo of myself with the sunset and twisted pine in the background. My earlier photos in Paris captured the random nostril, eyebrow or ear; however, this snapshot perfectly frames the glimmering Mediterranean and my face. And just as I was surprised by my dowdy appearance in the Boston airport shot, I'm equally surprised by the thoughtful woman looking back at me here. It's not just the tan, the leanness from miles of walking. Nor is it relaxation from several weeks of dream trip. After all, Mon Cher has abandoned me. No, I see strength, fulfilment. I see a confident woman who, no matter how she's tossed, lands on her feet, graceful as a cat.

The lingering light entices me to walk one more time down the cliffs to check email at the café. My change of plans delights my son who sent me on this trip. He writes, "Secretly, I'd been hoping this would happen ..." I write that I, too, am charmed by my unanticipated circumstances, that tomorrow I will stroll the Farmers' Market, that later I will translate a poem I've found in the local newspaper. Now the Café Sola bartender whistles Mozart's Concerto in G minor. What a marvelous place to be marooned. Robinson Crusoe never had it this good. ###

Chapter 19
Choosing Beggars

Teach me to feel another's woe ... – Alexander Pope

Late one afternoon in Collioure, I see an older man with a kindly, bearded face sitting on his valise by the entry to Notre Dame des Anges. He holds his knitted hat that contains about 30 cents. Though he speaks to me in French and blows me a kiss, I continue on my way to the jetty and the tiny shrine perched high on the cliff. The narrow walkway to the signal light is congested, so I decide to let the crowd thin before I explore it. I return to the church.

By the time I arrive, the man by the church door appears to be praying. I walk past him into the sanctuary, sit for a few minutes to contemplate the statuary, then I light a candle and leave. As I emerge from the dark church into the brilliant afternoon, the same man is crushing saltines with his feet and feeding the crumbs to the pigeons. This gesture so touches me, that even though I walk on, I turn around, walk back, and put five euros in his hat. He beams, thanks me in French, and blows another kiss. I tell him that the money is *"un cadeau des anges,* a gift from the angels." A few days later, I see The Pigeon Man near the Café Sola smoking and wonder how the angels and I feel about that. I had thought he'd buy food with his capful of coins, but almsgiving doesn't come with directives. Give. Let go. Period.

I remember my first day in Paris, a woman with Bambi eyes had silently extended her arm to offer tiny bouquets of *muguet des bois*, lily of the valley, tied with white thread. She smiled shyly from her seat on the curb. I smiled and walked past, but when I encountered the next dark-haired woman, also selling the *muguet des bois* in elfin bouquets, I stopped and bought one. If she offers something lovely, is she still begging? My interactions with beggars will perplex me for the remainder of my journey and probably for the rest of my life.

Although numerous beggars have approached me over the years in Boston, I had conveniently nudged them out of my mind before arriving in France. Paris teems with beggars quite unlike their aggressive American counterparts, at least in Boston, where they walk right up to you, rattle the paper cup with the hour's take, and dare you to refuse. In Paris, on the other hand, the beggars appeal to your emotions, your compassion – your guilt. My mind can't erase their images.

A gypsy mother on the sidewalk, her skirts fanned around her, cradling a child, maybe 6-7 years old, begging for food.

Another woman kneeling on the sidewalk, hands and head on the pavement in fashionable Saint-Germain-des-Prés, where smartly dressed people step around her and stride to Les Deux Magots where a sandwich costs nearly $30. Is her posture supplication for money? Is she praying?

Near Notre Dame, young Eastern European women engulf me and implore, "Speak English?" then thrust a handwritten letter in English, sometimes in a plastic sheath, into my face. The letter tells a dire tale of sick parents, dying children, money needed for an operation. A plea to assuage terrible things. If true.

Perhaps the most disconcerting mendicants are those who hover like shabby angels at the entrances of the grand cathedrals, who make me reassess my values each time I walk in. My faith tells me: "*inasmuch as ye have done it unto the least of these my brethren, ye have done it unto Me ...*" Yet I don't do anything for these nameless brothers and sisters. Instead, I marvel at stonework and colored glass, the decorative shell of my faith and walk right past the living, suffering heart of it. My faith also teaches me, "*be as wise as serpents and guileless as doves.*" If I do give, am I being holy – or hoodwinked?

And what about the middle-class men and women who rattle the paper cup? What's their story? While walking through the Latin Quarter, a well-dressed woman and children approached me. She said she was from Montreal and claimed "emergency" while waiting for money to be wired for – what was it? – a car problem? Theft? I sympathized profusely, suggested the embassy, and hurried away. She lunged to catch the next passerby. I could not so easily escape the young woman rattling a cup on the steps of St. Gervais church across from my hostel. She held her post for at least two days then disappeared.

Some beggars, on the other hand, are fixtures like the elderly, heavyset man with a cane who sat on the top step, right side, of the St. Paul metro in Paris. I saw him in May and he was still there in June. People spoke to him, dropped the occasional coin in his cup. What's his story? Does he actually gather any money there, the sunshine on his shoulders? Or does he draw energy from people rushing to their jobs? Does the roar of the rue de Rivoli make his day worth living? Does he spend the night there? If not, where does he go? Can he walk? Who was he in his life before he camped at the top of the metro stairs?

Perhaps the most important thing beggars demand from us is honesty to look at them and talk to them and realize, "that could be me." Perhaps we need these beggars, these people like loose fringe on the edges of our lives, to remind us that humanity is a single fabric of many strands, some more snugly woven in than others.

So, are the Parisian musicians also beggars, even if they offer something of value as they await appreciation? My first encounter happened on the train from Charles de Gaulle airport. A Latina chanteuse wearing old sneakers sang "La Bamba" with her karaoke machine. After a couple of numbers, she passed through my car with her tired eyes. I guess she didn't expect much because her change purse was so small. I didn't contribute, perhaps because I felt like a captive audience. Much later I would learn that these musicians are legitimate. The city of Paris actually auditions them and allows 300 to perform on the metro for our "tranquility." We are not obliged to pay for the music.

One day I listened to the tinny tunes of the grizzled pianist on the Pont Notre-Dame, bridge to the cathedral, and let the small audience of tourists plunk change in his small bucket. Another day, I, myself, dropped 1€ in the knitted toque of the *accordéoniste* who obliged me with *La Vie en Rose* as I gazed across the Seine. Painted actors posed like statues. Other actors draped in gold *lamé* tower like King Tut. All await our appreciation and generosity. Who else in my life awaits appreciation and generosity, typically without the coins and cup?

Now I regret I gave nothing to the old fellow sitting against a side door at Chartres Cathedral. He had offered his scallop shell, the sign of the pilgrim. Are pilgrims beggars, too?

So, we choose our beggars. We must decide with whom we will share: I choose the musicians, flower peddlers, and nonthreatening old men. Perhaps tomorrow I will choose differently, for beggars are not confined to the streets of Paris or cathedrals of France. I meet them every day in friends, family, strangers who require something of value from me, who ask me to believe their tales of need – both physical and spiritual – or who simply beseech with their eyes. Recognition. Appreciation. Generosity. Yes, I need these, too. Without sitting on the ground, extending my hat, I, too, am a beggar. ###

Chapter 20
Adieu, Collioure

There is nothing like a dream to create the future.
– Victor Hugo

My last day in Collioure, Market Day overtakes the town square. The now familiar jazz ensemble throbs under the babble of a hundred shoppers and vendors. I easily find my favorite green grocer and bread man in the throng of dizzying choices: crusty breads, fruits and vegetables from Languedoc and Spain, fresh flowers, oysters on ice, ribbon and elastic, wine, sandals, sacks of spices, pungent cheeses, filmy sarongs and floppy hats, candy, mounds of olives and more olives, sausages, gaping fish and pearly squid, jellies and honey, paella and meatballs to go. Aside from flaxseed bread, tomatoes, red bell pepper, carrots, apricots, and strawberries – greedy girl! – I severely limit my buying and wonder how I can still cram gifts into my luggage. Now I understand why serious backpackers cut the handles off their toothbrushes to save weight. Trundling home a bottle or two of local wine presents a logistic impossibility though cheese and textiles might fit.

Because I have no more room for souvenirs, I glance only casually at the array of bracelets, wallets, and textiles spread on the ground along the length of the boat launch canal, an impromptu flea market. When I hear a percussive, certainly non-Gallic cadence, I edge toward the speaker. "You speak English!" Chuck, a fireman from Vancouver, introduces me to the vendor from Senegal and seems eager to converse in English, as well.

We talk about the delights of Collioure, the sea, the market, the friendly vendors, even Boston. Then Chuck escorts me to meet Carol, an engaging fitness instructor with a face sculpted by an Italian master. Tomorrow she's off to Corsica. She promises to email and tell me about the island that I must forfeit due to the train strike. Like so many other women, she exclaims, "Good for you!" when I describe my solo journey. Yes, so far so good for me. Even without Mon Cher or a Chuck or any traveling companion these past weeks, good for me, the plucky wanderer.

I set my purchases on the sea wall to linger at the waterfront where *barques* tug and squeak at their moorings. Out near the jetty, the commandoes clamber over what looks like broken boats, then paddle furiously in kayaks. Beneath the *château*, the woodcutter has set out his carvings of boats and figurines just as he has every day. He smiles, eats, and keeps working under his umbrella. Just another day in Collioure, but now I recognize so many familiar faces. This very morning at Café Sola, Jo, the woman I met buying carrots, and her husband Dave, the *barque* painter, talk about the lure, the magic of the sea. The light hadn't been right for him to paint, neither bright nor stormy. Now rising wind threatens to blow off my tan, so I soak up a little more Mediterranean sunshine to wear home or at least to Paris. I scoop up my bags and hike back to my hotel.

Several hours later, after Mass at Our Lady of the Angels, a benediction for my journey, I head toward Café Sola for one last email check and a stirrup cup of sangria. All the clouds have blown away. The wind out of the north has dropped a little, yet continues to whip the sea into madness. Surging smoky turquoise swells backlit by translucent aqua thunder endlessly on the stony beach. So, too, my interior landscape surges with renewed energy and the bold, clear colors of Collioure. Even shadows cast by Mon Cher's abandonment cannot diminish them.

Certainly, I am not the first to fall under the spell of this place. Matisse, Picasso, and other Fauvist painters returned many times to paint these mountains, this sunshine, and this sea. More recently, Jo and Dave spent nearly 11 years making short visits from California because Americans don't have an automatic right to work in France. Howard from New York more easily untangled the snarls of red tape because his wife is French. Staying here for months at a time or living here year-round as an ex-pat seems nearly impossible, never mind the expense.

Yet for the past nine days, the teal blue sea has surged beneath me, just as I had imagined when I willed myself into that calendar seascape of Hawaii 10 years ago. Like Alice stepping through her looking glass, I stepped through the first calendar, then more calendars. Tropical calendars. Paris calendars. Every day for years. And the tiny tendril "what if ...?" coiled around my thoughts and never, never let go. I saved the old calendar pages in an envelope and, from time to time, retreated into turquoise possibility.

Perhaps more importantly, I shared my "what if" with soul mates who believed in my crazy idea. Their gifts – a journal, a hat, a scarf, a money belt, and guidebooks "to use in France" – sustained my courage, even when I had nearly lost hope. Now, thanks to them and a fortuitous train strike, I have filled my mind and soul with the roiling Mediterranean.

Filled. How often do we ever *really* have enough? Our fill? How often are we truly satisfied? Well, I am now. I gaze at the sea until the sun, red as a pomegranate, slides beneath the horizon, and I must secure my barn door shutters. Nine days of paradise for less than the cost of an ambulance ride. At least a few times in our lives we need "enough," a surfeit of something we crave be it chocolate, Mediterranean blue, free time, or love. We need to believe in our bliss to find it. For now, at least, I bask in turquoise contentment.

The next morning, I inhale cool, early air and blink away sea dazzle as I walk to the train station. My suitcase clatters over the cobblestones, the only sound save the slap of water against the sea wall. No one is up. The café tables sit empty, beaded with dew.

On the balustrade, I see the man I'd noticed several times in this very place, staring as if dazed by an old sorrow. He's very brown and portly now, but must have been blond and cherubic in his youth. His nondescript shirt and pants, heavy socks, and plaid bedroom slippers suggest that he is poor. He does not smell of alcohol, nor does he beg. He just stares at a point on the sidewalk, close to the sea wall.

Perhaps someone he loved was lost at sea – or somewhere else. Perhaps he, himself, is lost.

Until this morning, I was afraid to offer him cookies or strawberries as I did the woodcarver, in case he was mentally unstable and might follow me. But this morning, as I leave Collioure, I heed a little voice: *Give him some fruit.* I walk past him a few yards, fish around in my bag, then walk back and offer him a pear. He recoils in happy surprise and growls in jolly French something I can't understand about "*la pomme*! an apple!" At least his sad eyes brighten for a moment as he accepts my small gift.

At the train station, small clusters of travelers murmur in the sunshine. I photograph the determined little poppies that grow through crumbling cement beside the track. "They grow well in the wild but are hard to grow in a garden," someone tells me. Perhaps The Pear Man is like that.

Later, from my upper level train seat, I view with detachment this tawny inland landscape streaking past, a world of asparagus fields, vineyards, and olive groves. White horses graze in fields of red poppies. Yellow flowers mass beside the rails. No sea colors here. Only two hours ago, I left Collioure, yet already I wonder: *Did I dream it? Fall into a fairy tale?*

Behind me, a cashmere-voiced mother explains the world to her toddler. "The sign says, Montpelier. Some people will get off the train, and some will get on ... I don't know where they are going." Now *Maman* reads to her daughter: "*neige,* snow ... *pomme,* apple ... *morte,* dead ... *prince* ..." Snow White? A fairy tale. Timeless stories of imagination and truths. May this little girl never outgrow them. ###

Chapter 21
Sleeping with Strangers: The Hostel Experience

There are no strangers here; only friends you haven't yet met.
– W.B. Yeats

Bunk with strangers? Who might rob me or worse? OK, so I've been uneasy about staying in hostels on the trip, even though it's the only way on my squeeze-the-buffalo-off-the-nickel budget. But students do this all the time for days and weeks. Surely, I can do it for a few nights and be secure, despite some scary hostel movie my kids rant about. After all, hadn't I slept with strangers when I was 21? Back then, when I was job hunting in Cambridge, Massachusetts, I booked myself into the YWCA in Central Square, hangout for hippies, political radicals, and starving students. To save money, I took one of eight beds in the "dorm" for only $1 a night, an hour's wage in those days. The long room had cubbies for our things, but my trust didn't stretch that far. I wanted to have my purse, a huge leather shoulder bag, close to me. Just in case. I crawled into bed with the shoulder bag, wrapped the strap around my leg, and slept fine. This strategy served me well during my hostel overnight in Iceland. Surely, I can do this again in metropolitan Paris.

The massive wooden door at 11 rue de Fauconnier once protected the inhabitants of a 17th century mansion. Today it protects penny-pinching grandmas like me. This hostel,

Maison Internationale des Jeunesses et Etudiantes, (MIJE) is tucked behind l'Hôtel de Ville, City Hall, in the heart of Paris. I buzz to be allowed in then pull open the towering hulk of an oak and wrought iron door that must weigh half a ton. Oops. I trip over the metal threshold, bounce my suitcase, and find myself in an entryway of heavy, exposed wooden beams and terra cotta floor tile. Long, weathered tables with heavy chairs fill both sides of the space. Tall French windows let in light from the courtyard and keep the room from being oppressive. Velvet doublets and pantaloons would not be out of place here.

The dark-eyed clerk sits behind a wooden counter where the green glass shade of her desk lamp gleams like a votive in the dimness. She searches for my name and once she finds it, I realize I have been holding my breath. Now I exist.

I have scored a single room, but on the sixth floor with no lift. *"Monter! Seul escalier.* Climb! There are only the stairs." I lug my suitcase, laptop, camera, and purse up the winding oaken staircase, often leaning against the massive oaken banister and wrought iron rail to rest. The feet of centuries have worn the wood underfoot slightly concave. Up. Up. Still up. My quivering arms stretch back to length on the several landings, well-lit by more long windows facing a leafy courtyard.

After 99 stairs – yes, I counted – I find myself in Cinderella's garret and swing open the six-foot tall windows. There are no screens to compromise my view. Dollops of cloud drift east across the rooftops of Paris. From my sixth story vantage point, turrets, pointed roofs, and

144

exotic spires rise from cream-colored stone buildings in ancient, haphazard design. By contrast, the formal garden in the courtyard below blooms with restful restraint: angular hedges of boxwood, triangular beds of pink rhododendron, a profusion of red and orange roses near an ornate street lamp. A grove of pollarded sycamores offers a haven for scores of birds who chirp incessantly. Pigeons coo on the nearby slate roofs. Only the Montparnasse skyscraper to the south pulls me out of the 17th century. I am infused with romance, even without fickle Mon Cher.

I explore my tiny shower and sink, then the shared water closet about the size of an airplane toilet in the hall outside my door. The ubiquitous pink toilet tissue, flat and narrower than ours, reminds me that the French have smaller *derrières*.

MIJE lodging, so cheap and ideally situated in the center of Paris, is a hit with school groups as well as solitary travelers of all ages. Stays are limited to just a few days at a time to avoid semi-permanent residents. In short, bookings are hard to come by. I manage to secure a couple of days in each of their three properties in the Marais neighborhood, so a few days later I check in at the hostel on rue de Fourcy, a pedestrian street. This building is a half-timbered Tudor with a modern marvel, an elevator. The red elevator door has a doorknob and swings open like a closet.

To save money, I now share a room: four women with two bunk beds. My convivial Brazilian roommates, 30-ish, tell me not only where to find the best ice cream, but also how to find a Wi-Fi connection in the courtyard below where young soccer players kick balls against Saint-Gervais church. That evening street sounds bounce off the stones of the church, instead of balls. Against a background of conversation from the sidewalk cafes, I hear the muted roar of traffic along the Seine, the bells of Notre Dame, a revved motorcycle, and the urgent the hee-haw, hee-haw of the police cars.

By 10:30 p.m., no roommates have appeared. From the café outside, I catch some boozy singing in French. I carefully climb the ladder to my bunk, tuck my laptop and purse under the covers, then tie my cameras to the far rail. (Incredibly, my Canon that traveled to England found me in St. Denis just an hour before I left.) Even if I don't know who is sleeping in the bunk beneath me, I feel secure. Such is trust. Either I believe in the basic goodness of people and take a few precautions to keep honest people honest, or I live a narrow life in fear. Once I put in a single earplug, I fall into peaceful sleep.

In the wee hours, I float to consciousness as an Indian-looking woman emerges from the lower bunk and closes the window to shut out the noise. So much for fresh air. I drift back to sleep and wake with the light to Daniela's ladylike snoring in Portuguese. She purrs.

My three roommates still sleep, but I'm ready for coffee. Exuberant children's voices the night before suggest a school group has arrived. Sure enough, I follow the chatter toward the dining room with heavy beams where 50 kiddos wake me up along with my *café*.

For a while, I watch how 9-year-olds attack baguettes: pull open and spread jam, or slice neatly and spread jam, or twist into bits. A young boy with glasses stares at his cocoa mug as though he'd lost something. Aha! He fishes out soggy baguette with his spoon and slurps it up.

Since all the tables are filled, two shy little girls sit with me. They do not speak English, so I tell them in French that I am a teacher in the United States. Eyes widen. A foreigner! One little nose drips, so I offer a *mouchoir*, a tissue. She uses it immediately.

I intercept one of the teachers as she passes and enjoy a little conversation, partly English, mostly French. She and her husband, another teacher, are chaperoning this group from near Mont-Blanc on a four-day tour of her native Paris. She grew up in Montmartre. We exchange addresses and invitations to visit each other. She would love to show me her Paris – and she means it as evidenced by her sincere email a few days later.

Back in the dorm room, my bunkmate is up. She looks about 50 and does not smile or speak. I introduce myself, anyway, learn that her name is Elizabeth, and she speaks no English. She breakfasts from her cache of Ensure and grapes while the young women from Brazil pack to leave for Germany and chirp wishes for a good journey. Their cheer fills the room like a fragrance. Already I miss them.

The next morning, I'm in the dining room under massive ancient beams, crowded this time with students ages 11-14 from Carcassonne. The only available seat faces my taciturn bunkmate Elizabeth. Again, I try again to initiate conversation, and this time she warms up, though she speaks with an accent I find hard to understand. By now, I am on to a third full cup of coffee, and Elizabeth has become talkative. She tells me that she is from Guadeloupe, Caraïbes, works for La Poste and travels. She has a man in Venice and points to a gobstopper of a ring, evidently a gift from her lover. With little preamble, she says she wants to spend the day with me. I thank her and tell her that I needed to write. She backs right off.

Then she asks if I am "*Catholique*." I say "yes," so much simpler than explaining my personal faith journey. She launches into an animated monologue then looks at me questioningly. One of the teachers from Mont-Blanc helps to interpret: Tomorrow, Sunday, she wants me to accompany her to the Church of the Miraculous Medal where tradition holds that the Virgin has appeared. I had planned to go to St. Sulpice to hear the renowned organ, but sure, I'll go.

"Oui, je vous accompagnerai. Merci bien."

She seems pleased in a brisk way and walks away. Later, as the church bells ring in the steeple of St. Gervais, just across the cobblestones, Elizabeth stands at the hostel window facing the church and crosses herself. I think I can trust her – and trust my judgment. Isn't that what this trip is all about? ###

Chapter 22
Saints Among Us

"...no butterfly interest, but a real love which is worthy of the name, which is capable of the dignity of sacrifice."
– Celia Thaxter

Elizabeth and I had agreed to leave for Mass at 9 a.m., yet by 8:30 she has already eaten, put on her dress, plus heels and jewelry, then returned downstairs to urge me on. So much for my second cup of coffee. I sigh, then rush to bandage the half-dollar sized blister on the sole of my foot. Despite her brusqueness, Elizabeth means well; she knows that I want to catch the organ concert at St. Sulpice at 11 a.m.

My companion walks briskly. I have trouble keeping up with her because of the blister and wonder why she wants a companion if she's running a footrace. We descend into the St. Paul metro under a mist of rain, only to emerge a few minutes later to *"le déluge."* Water cascades down the stairs of the Sèvres-Babylone metro, while a worker squeegees, a futile exercise against the flood. Elizabeth chats in French to the clerk behind the ticket window who offers her a forgotten umbrella.

I pull out my thin plastic poncho from the Dollar Store, my hedge against showers and bedbugs. *Quelle merveille!* What a marvel. The ladies have never seen such a thing. I smirk. Imagine! I'm setting a fashion trend in Paris in cheap *plastique*. The rain falls more gently now, but time is short. We dash the last blocks to the Chapel of the Miraculous Medal, Elizabeth plowing walkers aside with her new umbrella. I limp along in her wake.

A new building dating to the 1930s, the chapel seems modern, light, and glittery compared with the dimly lit medieval churches darkened by time I have already visited. Here, mosaics of childlike blonde angels adorn walls encrusted with fragments of silver, blues, and gold – a dreamscape. Filigree balconies and windows lining the nave lend a refreshing airiness to the sanctuary.

Immediately, I sense a difference beyond architecture: more piety, more devotion. For instead of simply praying in their chairs before Mass, believers place expensive bouquets of fresh tulips, roses, and lilies on the altar then prostrate themselves – not typical Sunday worship behavior. Fashionable women in expensive jewelry, weary women in polyester pants, teenagers in mini-skirts and golden sandals, they lie on the floor beneath the focal point of the chapel, a statue of the Virgin wearing a blue cloak and crown of stars. The man in rain-soaked jeans lies very still; asleep or entranced, I cannot tell. Elizabeth kneels and prays for about 15 minutes, lips moving, eyes closed. Eventually, we find chairs near the back, Mass begins, and I try to follow the rapid French. Loaves and fishes? I understand a little.

After the Mass, I see them. Two glass coffins, their edges sealed with golden metal like Snow White's coffin in the Disney film, rest on either side of the altar about chest high. Within each reposes a body dressed in a long, dark gray

150

habit and white headdress that that looks like a flying gull. Women? The headdress suggests as much. The smooth faces have a grayish cast. Wax? Or preserved human flesh?

I walk closer to the less crowded coffin on the left, and before I determine whether the figure is wax or real, Elizabeth hisses, *"Allez! Allez!* Go! Go!" The next Mass begins shortly. We exit, cutting across long lines waiting to enter the sanctuary, then almost jogging, we head toward St. Sulpice, a place Elizabeth has never been. She checks directions with a Croix Rouge, Red Cross, worker soliciting donations; however, he steers us toward Saint-Germain-des-Prés – the wrong direction. Now 20 minutes later, we retrace our route yet again, my raw blister stinging with each step. At least the rain has stopped.

After 30 minutes of walking, we find St. Sulpice tucked behind much scaffolding. For about ten minutes, I listen to the fabled organ play *mezzo-piano, pianissimo,* barely demonstrating its range and volume. Perhaps in the next movement … but my impatient companion taps her foot and clearly wants to be off. We rush back to the St. Paul's metro stop where she makes a phone call then excuses herself to meet a friend. All that rushing and following her – for what? We could have parted at the church, so I could have heard the rest of the organ concert. Elizabeth asks a passerby to snap photos, mumbles a quick *"au revoir,"* and leaves me on the sidewalk. I don't even know her last name.

Already it's an hour past checkout time at MIJE and I begin to fear that I am locked out of the building. I buzz five times, and though I am let in, I alarm one of the upstairs staff, a young man carrying laundry.

"*Arretez!* Stop!"

"*Je suis désolée.* I am so sorry. I was late. I am leaving. I am sorry."

"*D'accord.* OK." He nods curtly but does not smile.

I snatch my gear from the dorm room and rush out onto the cobblestones. Within a few minutes, I slide into the now familiar Café Louis Philippe for pesto ravioli. Off my feet, my throbbing blister no longer stings me. I sip espresso, watch the leisurely sidewalk traffic, reflect upon my excursion with Elizabeth, and reaffirm why I prefer to travel alone. Sure, I wasted a lot of time and energy this morning, but the church intrigued me, especially the two corpses and the homage they inspired.

Much later I learn that not only are the two nuns real, but I was, indeed, in the presence of a canonized saint, St. Catherine Labouré, The Saint of Silence, and never knew it. Aside from the effusive adoration of believers, nothing seemed out of the ordinary: I had no spiritual experience, perceived no aura or supernatural phenomena. No profound thoughts. No special effects. No razzle-dazzle. No Shazam! Only the throng of those paying homage caused me to wonder: *Why?* And I ponder the nature of sainthood.

Many of those recognized as saints reveal their godliness through daring, often militant, acts of raw courage, like St. Michel wielding his protective sword. Other saints endure martyrdom like St. Joan of Arc, burned at the stake, or St. Stephen, stoned to death by a mob. Sometimes the Catholic

Church catches a person being good and canonizes him or her.

Yet other more obscure saints look like anyone else. We walk right past them because they are everywhere, performing their duties fueled by quiet devotion that never brags and never quits. Saints love and endure for the long haul, even an invisible "Saint of Silence" like Catherine Labouré. Many more "saints" elude recognition simply because they are so engrossed in their missions of love. I number these saints among my friends: women like Deb and Claudette who for years cared for husbands ravaged by cancer; Terry who cares for her granddaughter whose mom is in rehab; my own mother, a staunch beacon for Dad who foundered in the fog of Alzheimer's disease. Anonymous caregivers are legion. Perhaps the true miracle and mystery of saints is their perseverance when devotion doesn't make rational sense, when there is no logical "payoff."

Young Catherine Labouré had been in the convent only a few months when she claimed the Virgin Mary asked her to create what came to be known as "The Miraculous Medal." Catherine's bishop believed the postulant and produced the medal, which then became associated with many healings during the cholera epidemic of 1832. Catherine's role, however, remained secret until after her death.

The popular medallion still circulates as jewelry, key chains, even decoration for diaper pins. Perhaps we need these tokens to focus our beliefs because as humans, we're touchers. We still depend on our finite senses to prepare us for the infinite world of spirit. Whether we accept Catholic theology and the sainthood of these two women or not, their bodies provide a powerful reminder that yes, we will die, and yes, we can do a lot of good before we do. Veneration, shrines, medals, saints – all focus our capricious human attention span on something beyond the here and now, something eternal. We crave that reassurance, especially the Claudettes, the Terries, the Debs who love the hardest, the longest with so little recognition.

Fortunately, someone recognized St. Catherine and St. Louise de Marillac, on the other side of the altar, and started the process of canonization; these women had good PR. We venerate them as saints because we need to remember and retell their stories to encourage ourselves. We also need to remember that any one of us is capable of going beyond our personal best, capable of persevering against all logic – in short, capable of miracles. Saints, it seems, dare better than the rest of us to become their finest selves. ###

Chapter 23
Living on Faith and Caramel *Crêpes*

Forget not to show love [hospitality] unto strangers:
Thereby some have entertained angels unawares.
– Hebrews 13:2

I wait for the click. Nothing. I have already opened the hostel door several times within the hour, but this time the swipe card does not work. *Pas de problème.* A slender woman had entered our suite just as I left to stow my bag downstairs. I rap on the door and within moments, the Caribbean roommate opens it, smiles graciously, and in French explains how to use the card. Though I know perfectly well how to open the darn door, I accept her kind instructions. Thus, I met Fatima. Doors. Sometimes they hide new friends.

The next morning, Fatima inquires whether I have slept well, then spies my bare feet. "Ooh, aren't you cold?" she asks. Touched by her concern, I assure her that I am fine and continue to dress for breakfast. Meanwhile, she offers a card to our third roommate, a young Korean woman who regards her with genuine puzzlement. "It's a prayer," said Fatima. "For you." Again, the generous smile. By the time I leave for my *petit déjeuner*, breakfast, Fatima is sitting on the lower bunk with her beige scarf over her head, apparently reading the Bible.

The dining room has emptied, and I am just finishing my coffee, when I recognize the beige scarf, now looped around Fatima's neck. A jaunty golf cap squelches the irrepressible Afro, a few wayward strands sprung free. A loose cotton jacket, bubble hem skirt over leggings, and flats, all neutral tones, complete her flowing ensemble. Her life, I would soon learn, is as comfy and unstructured as her clothing. I gesture for her to join me, and as she claims her English is poor, we begin to converse in French. She speaks slowly and listens intently like someone who wants to keep the conversation going. Despite our language differences, we seem to understand each other, at least most of the time.

At first, we talk about Paris and how much we like the hostel and the generous breakfast. "It's all I will eat today." She smiles. "I have just one meal." I ask if she is a student.

She chuckles. "*Non*! What age do you think I am?"

"25?"

"Higher."

"35? ... 40?"

"Higher ..." The mischievous smile.

"No! You're kidding."

"I'm 42 ..." Young enough to be my daughter. I tell her that I am 62.

"... but you do not look that old, maybe 55."

We talk about her two children and my four, then she explains that she is living by her faith after escaping an abusive relationship. We talk candidly as strangers often do.

"Did your husband hurt you?" I venture.

"Not in my body, but in my mind." She becomes animated describing life with her controlling man. "He was a dictator. I could not have the dinner one minute late!" She speaks rapidly for many minutes, and though I cannot translate as quickly, I know she describes the day she had reached the end of her endurance. Before she could harm herself, she said, she discovered The Lord who protected her. "He saved my life." Now she is safe. Beloved. Free. As soon as her children could fend for themselves, Fatima left her marriage to live in Paris, sometimes with her children, sometimes in hostels. In July and August, she stays with relatives in the country "with meadows and horses." For this she pays nothing. *"Mon Seigneur m'aidera.* My Lord takes care of me." Her face glows with the passion of a gentle fanatic.

She doesn't know where she will sleep tonight, yet Fatima's serenity convinces me that a bed is of little consequence. She just needs to make a couple of phone calls. Something will turn up. *"Dieu y pourvoira.* God will provide," she insists. I know that our hostel is full this evening, so months ago I had booked a two-star hotel near the Louvre. It crosses my mind to invite her to join me. Just as quickly, I decide against it, ashamed that I cannot trust as blithely as she does.

Fatima wraps her leftover baguette in a paper napkin and tucks it into her purse.

"What will you do today?" she asks.

"Oh, just enjoy springtime in Paris, the sun, the Seine, the flowers, and check out Shakespeare and Company." She has

157

never heard of the iconic bookstore, despite her many years in the city, so we agree to spend the morning exploring together. On the easy walk from the hostel past Notre Dame, I notice right away that she walks much faster than I can.

In the unpretentious bookstore, Fatima gazes in wonderment as though visiting a museum. She moves deliberately, pausing as something catches her eye: aged wooden floor and beams; books crammed floor to ceiling into every dusty crevice; battered chairs, plush theatre seats, benches. She spends extra time reading the soul-baring messages scrawled by visitors and pinned dense as feathers on a notice board. I point to a sign painted in black block letters over a small doorway: *Be not inhospitable to strangers/Lest they be angels in disguise*. She nods, "*C'est vrai.* That's true." Her smiles signal enchantment with the shabby comfort of the upstairs library, a word lover's haven. "I'll come back here to read all of these!" She scans the room, "and be out of the rain."

Fatima enquires about the free lecture that evening, but as the scheduled writer prides himself on his graphic violence, I decline. "No matter. There will be others. I am so blessed that you brought me here. Now, I would like to show you Paris. I will be your guide." And since she is so cordial, I accept.

First, we will walk to the beautiful medieval Musée de Cluny to save metro fare. Located near the Sorbonne, the medieval gardens offer inviting, shady spaces along the approach to the museum. Low wicker fencing edges the

Unicorn Forest. I am reading the description of the Garden of Love when Fatima asks, "Would you like to go inside the museum?"

"No, thanks. It's too expensive."

"I will pay for you."

I consider her one meal a day and uncertain lifestyle and, despite her cell phone, figure she has little money. "No, really, but thank you."

"And why not?"

How not to offend? "Because it's too beautiful to be inside on a sunny day in Paris!" True enough.

"Ah ... most Americans I meet want the museums and churches. 'Museums and churches.' You are different ..." Her smile makes the remark a compliment.

After we stroll the gardens, I suggest coffee. "Later. You like flowers, so first I would like to show you Parc André Citroën away from the tourists. You will enjoy it, I think." Power walking to keep abreast of her, we zigzag along side streets and through tunnels in *le métro* where she pays my fare then emerge in a totally new neighborhood for me, the 15th arrondissement. Now the Eiffel Tower, usually west of me, soars in the east. And such a park! We wander down shady *alleés* amidst fluttering leaves. Roses abound. We pass young professionals eating sack lunches or smoking in the first hot sunshine of spring. "The people who work in offices come here," Fatima explains.

Fountains at the southern end of the lawn shoot jets of water straight into the sky, and a squealing toddler runs barefoot through the spray. Fatima splashes water on her face and never stops smiling. Behind us, a hot air balloon bobs at its tether, and as promised, not a postcard vendor or any vendor, for that matter, in sight. I have escaped the tourist scene.

After a sunny stroll past undulating tall grasses and color-themed gardens – blue, green, orange, red, silver, and gold – symbolizing the planets, even the indefatigable Fatima agrees it is time for a snack, so we stop at a sidewalk café. Since it is Wednesday, school is closed for instruction. Instead, the day is devoted to extra-curricular activities. Little boys about 6 years old in t-strap shoes, kick a soccer ball with hilarious abandon off a nearby wall. We keep a lookout lest it bounce off our table. They are so joyous no one shoos them away, not even the waiter wrapped in his white apron who pretends to scold, then waggles a finger and laughs, clearly sharing their springtime enthusiasm.

Fatima orders *crêpes au caramel,* and I order a cup of espresso and two golf-ball-sized *boules* of ice cream, chocolate and raspberry. When I insist upon paying, Fatima interprets this as another of God's blessings. "You know," she says, "I had been dreaming of a caramel *crêpe* … how good it would taste. And now, *voila*! I have a *crêpe.* God is good!" We share stories of Providence: the money, the clothes, the people, the opportunities that arrived precisely when we needed them – probably because we never quit trusting or believing ourselves to be worthy of love and assistance.

I tell about raising my four children alone and the $100 bills that arrived in envelopes with no return address, the sacks of clothes left on my porch, the baskets of food, the insightful conversation with someone I scarcely knew when I had reached a teetering point. Now I have met someone who trusts the future, the ambiguity of the unknown as I do. My new friend, Fatima, is both childlike and wise.

All too soon, I need to collect my baggage at the hostel and check in at my new hotel in another arrondissement. Perhaps, I should have confirmed the reservation that morning. *Eh bien*, too late now. Still, I feel a frisson of uneasiness that my room will be cancelled if I am late. We hurry to the metro, transfer at Montparnasse, and struggle through shoulder-to-shoulder crowds at St. Michel station. Fatima nimbly hops onto the train as the doors begin to close. She grabs my hand and pulls hard. The doors squeeze harder. I let go. Now the door seal clamps her fingers, still stretching out to me. She gestures furiously with her other hand. *Stay? Go? Where? What!* Then she is gone.

I wait for several minutes, but no train arrives. Nor do I know exactly where it would take me, anyway. I climb dim stairs out of the metro, back into the brilliance of spring and walk to the hostel. There, about an hour later, Fatima and I find each other and trade sequels to our abrupt separation. I have to hurry to my new hotel; she needs to meet her children for dinner. We agree to meet for dinner the next night, so she gives me her number on a mock euro, printed with a Christian message, the same one she had handed our Korean roommate. By the next night, however, I have walked another huge blister onto my heel. I phone Fatima to reschedule, but she has commitments until my flight home. I never see her again.

So often, though, I think of the Fatimas who like doves thrive on the crumbs of Paris. Like a child, she trusts her faith to provide for her. And it does. Crazy? I don't think so. How much more sensible for her to depend on a gracious God, as saints and mystics do, than to trust an abusive spouse. She's also quick to recognize – and give thanks – when her simple needs are met, whether *crêpes au caramel* or a shabby bookstore haven. No, Fatima isn't crazy at all. In her offbeat, hand-to-mouth existence, Fatima expects the best – and finds it. Her optimism is her security, a currency almost universally accepted. Fatima refreshes and blesses those fortunate enough to befriend her. ###

Chapter 24
Chez Simone, "Poor but Free"

I know who I am and who I may be, if I choose. -- Miguel de
Cervantes, *Don Quixote*

The front door of Simone's Paris apartment stands
ajar. Poor security? No, the door jams against the
stone flagging and opens barely 18 inches. I twist my
suitcase and body through the gap and ring the first bell I
see - then reassure the bewildered man who opens the door
that I am *confuse*. I look again at my instructions, realize that
Simone's B&B is on the sixth floor, and head to the lift, a
filigreed metal cage, its floor the size of a bath mat. By
pulling the outside accordion metal doors and pushing the
wooden framed screen doors, I squash myself and *mes
bagages* inside the contraption. The eerily slow, creaky
ascent gives me time to count floors. At the sixth, I clumsily
extricate myself as doors slam behind me. Now in the
narrow passage, I face another two doors and do not
recognize either last name. I ring the left bell first. White-
haired Simone appears and, with few words and a tired
smile, ushers me into her flat. I had hoped for a more
effusive welcome.

Humble furnishings, bits of clutter, and gnarled plants
on the windowsill remind me that I am in someone's
longtime home, perhaps someone in reduced
circumstances. My room, just off her dining area, overlooks

a park teeming with noisy children playing soccer and riding bicycles. Close to the glass balcony door, a floor lamp and armchair under shelves of books create an inviting space; a tiny table holds water, a small electric pot, instant coffee, and teas. One step up, separate from the reading space, the double bed mounded with colorful pillows faces the balcony. I wonder whether Simone has given me her bed. In this tiny flat, where does she sleep? In the kitchen?

Still reserved, Simone shows me the bathroom, brilliant in natural light, mirrors, and plants. She inclines her head, "All for you." Her few bathroom articles are stacked on a tiny chest of drawers outside the door. While I situate myself, Simone offers to "cook" tea and serves it in my room with a pre-packaged biscuit, then she returns to her ironing in the dining area. I feel like an intruder.

Eh bien ... I'll catch up on correspondence. Simone tells me that her Internet is down and though her son lives nearby, he's too busy to come today to fix it. She says I can connect to Wi-Fi in the park, but my blister will not allow me to walk that far to explore just yet. I write a few postcards while I finish my tea, then decide that I must establish some rapport with this withdrawn woman in whose home I will sleep.

Over her ironing board, I initiate conversation. She cannot escape. Simone asks me nothing about myself, perhaps respecting my privacy and allowing me to set the tone of our interaction. She continues ironing and speaks carefully in English, "because I always talk to guests in English." Sometimes she finishes her brief replies with a slow, pretty smile. I think she is comfortable with me. Her restrained responses, like maxims, lead me to think that she is German, but I don't say this. No, she was born here in Paris and has been here since she finished her studies decades ago. I estimate that she is in her late 70s. She volunteers that she had been married for 26 years, then sighs. "That was long enough."

The many photos tacked to the apartment walls intrigue me: jewel-colored birds and my hostess, relaxed, tan, smiling, in a tropical landscape. I ask about them. Simone stops ironing with a faraway gleam in her eyes and begins to describe the Foja Wilderness in Indonesia, one of the last wild places on earth. She's fascinated with the birds in the Mamberamo Mountains and wants to photograph them before they become extinct. Hosting B&B guests has funded her winter sojourns there these past eight years.

"How did you find this place?"

She continues ironing. "You will think I am silly, but I had wanted to go to Antarctica." A slow smile begins to soften her stern features. "At the time, I was working for a woman, a nasty woman, who said, 'You will never go to Antarctica!'" Simone sets down her iron and moves toward the world map. "I told her, 'Very well, then! I will go *here*!'" She suddenly sweeps her arm across the map and points: Foja Wilderness in Indonesia. She had never heard of it.

But she went. Amazing how our stubbornness directs us to passions unfulfilled.

Perhaps I talk a bit too much about how I admire women with a goal, a mission after age 60. Simone irons the sleeve of a cotton blouse and shrugs. "*C'est normal.* No biggie." Yet, photos taken in the Foja Wilderness show a stunningly beautiful white-haired woman, smiling, at ease with the natives. Simone? It has to be Simone. Without her heavy, tinted glasses she looks years younger. But it wasn't just the glasses, it was being at one with her beloved tropical wilderness, this kaleidoscope of birds and lush flowers, without the burden of being a B&B hostess. She tells me with quiet dignity, "I am poor, but I have my freedom." I cannot doubt for a moment that she is mistress of her own destiny.

When Simone goes out a few hours later, I immerse myself in a deep, hot bath and soak in both warmth and dazzling light, for the small bathroom has three large mirrors in addition to a window with a view of the sky. What did she say? "Light is important." Another maxim. To complete my indulgence, I've poured a glass of the sangria I found under the tea table. Apparently, the alcoholic offerings have been open for a while, maybe months, because it tastes like raisins. I empty my glass in the sink.

Revived, I apply a fresh bandage to my blister and strike out to explore the neighborhood. I find a tiny shop selling Comté, rusks, and Minervois – a light supper – and a Wi-Fi connection in the park where *le football* mania reigns. Perhaps my hostess has cast a pall on my outlook; the neighborhood doesn't feel as cozy as Hélène's.

The next morning, sunlight spills onto the small kitchen table she has set for one. While I sip my coffee and nibble cheese and a croissant, she works nearby at her computer.

Not wishing to interrupt her, I alternately gaze through the glass balcony door to the park and discreetly observe my surroundings. My subdued hostess has cordoned off her tiny personal space with screens, colorful Navajo rugs, and fringed blankets attached to a clothes line, rather like a yurt in the apartment. The kitchen seems to be behind her sleeping quarters. When she pulls back one of the blankets to get more coffee, I spy her narrow bed and lots of books on shelves that run the length of it. Resourceful, yet a hard way to make a living if you crave privacy as she clearly does.

The next day I want to go somewhere quiet and beautiful without hordes of tourists. Simone suggests the Rodin Museum. She reviews her schedule for the next day, anticipating that her guests will arrive early, perhaps even before I have left. "I hate that," she mumbles. Then she rereads her paperwork from the B&B agency. "*Three* guests. I hate that."

Though she had invited me to accompany her to the garden market this morning, she now has too much to do and grumbles about stock photos of birds. She shares that she worked last night until nearly 1 a.m. "Retirement" isn't part of her lexicon. Perhaps by way of apology for ditching me, she takes time to show me an online video of Sunday singing and dancing in the rue Mouffetard in the Latin Quarter. Her male friend, 70-ish, plays accordion accompaniment while another friend sings Piaf for the tourists. Golden years, indeed! Except for the reticence, Simone is my kind of lady. Pushing 80, fully engaged in life and adventure, living on her own terms, "poor but free," Simone is a model of who I wish to be. ###

Chapter 25
"Adorable Wrinkles": Beauty Revisited

"When grace is joined with wrinkles, it is adorable.
There is an unspeakable dawn in happy old age."
– Victor Hugo

A Parisian face keeps floating through my consciousness. It's the older woman I saw on a Montmartre bus, and she claims more mental headroom than the Basilica of the Sacré-Coeur. Why? Because of the way she held her head. I think that proud carriage on a woman about 80 years old spoke volumes about who she was or, at least, considers herself to be. She had huge pale bags under her green eyes fringed with mascaraed lashes; cheeks wrinkled like last October's apple; hair a deliberate brown ... but she was a *grande dame.* Those wrinkled cheeks were lightly powdered, her red lipstick fresh, not running, even in the 5 p.m. heat. Her earrings with dozens of tiny olive and brown marbles like bunched grapes jingled on her ears. She wore a milk chocolate brown over blouse woven with sheer patches. I don't remember the rest of her *costume* because I was focused on that head, her chin slightly elevated.

Who is she? Was she? An actress? Model? Ballerina? One could have been put off by her *hauteur,* except that she smiled very kindly at some teenagers who stood near her. I left the bus before she did, but she hasn't left me. Dylan

Thomas would approve her chic "rage against the dying of the light."

My own rage against aging began about 20 years ago when my hairdresser suggested a rinse to cover gray hair I had barely noticed for lack of mirror time while raising my four small children. Since I had borne my youngest at almost 38, and could possibly be mistaken for – dear, me – her grandmother, I invested in a box of hair color and applied it while the children napped. Trina woke early that afternoon and found me wearing what looked like molasses and plastic bag on my head.

"What's that?" she demanded.

"Special shampoo, honey."

She looked me straight in the eye, regarded the gummy plastic bag with arch skepticism, then announced, "I want something to eat."

A few years later, I decided that frosting, a permanent process, would blend the gray more naturally and save time – and questions. Besides, I could do it myself. No matter how much I wanted to rage against the dying of the light, I should not have attempted hair color while raging at my kids. This unfortunate day, a rush of adrenaline and high blood pressure induced by childish ingratitude, lost clothing, and quarrels drove me to escape to the bathroom. Instead of applying the frosting mixture wisp by delicate wisp, I slapped it on like mustard on a hot dog. The results were much the same. Instead of shimmering highlights of pale gold framing my face, I now had hanks of Big Bird yellow.

Not to worry. The bleach compound simply hadn't been on long enough to frost properly. Wiping away tears from the fumes, I mixed up another batch, choked a little, reapplied and waited.

No change.

My heart began to race as the kids pounded on the door. I assured them that "the stink" was OK and grabbed a bottle of my usual rinse to cover the ghastly mistake. I still don't know enough about alchemy to understand why blonde rinse on a yellow patch turned Lucille Ball orange, but I did know that I looked nothing like the young, carefree woman on the coloring kit box.

At supper, I wore my wooly hat to the table. The kids sensed that asking questions was not a good idea. After the strained meal, we shot to the grocery store to find a rinse with ash tones, reputed to cool down the red ones. Later, as I washed off the last-chance rinse, my fascinated 6-year-old pondered, "What if it turns purple?" I muttered that I wouldn't go to work. Fortunately, the result leaned less toward purple than to startling redhead.

The next morning, I slunk to work but not before one of my more observant colleagues winked and caroled, "Oh, I see SOMEBODY'S done something to her HAY-er!" All heads swiveled in my direction. During coffee break, I slipped away to my hairdresser cum chemist who for $20 gave me hair color that generated no comment and grew out within a year.

Perhaps I would have colored my hair forever had I not met Mon Cher with his lustrous silvery hair drawn back into an attractive ponytail. My hairdresser had already suggested a lighter shade of color as my elder hair began its slow fade. Perhaps now I can go gray with confidence, even without the graying sweetheart. I watch for tattletale roots, but none emerge. I'm as naturally platinum as I was when I was two. Boldly letting my hair grow out turned into a lovely surprise, rather like tearing out an old shag carpet and finding parquetry. My granddaughter tells me that my hair is "the color of the moon." I agree. I don't need to rage against the dying of the light. At this stage of my life, I reflect it.

Hair is easy to disguise. Not so my face. I remember that English composition assignment my first year of college: describe your face or your room in 500 words, double-spaced. After class, I took a hard look at the puzzled form in the mirror and studied a ripple of ash blonde hair draped over my high forehead, two thick eyebrows perched above worried green eyes, a Swedish nose, and under-bite. I decided I'd get more mileage out of my dorm room.

Over the years, my face enjoyed spurts of attention, usually during make-up sessions for amateur theatricals, fake eyelashes and all. More often, though, I forgot my face as I caromed off the walls of my life raising the four kiddos. During one of my first Empty Nest years, with my estrogen banging on Empty, I happened to glance in the mirror while I was headed somewhere else – and stopped dead. *Who the heck are YOU?"* I demanded of the washed-out woman who should have been my reflection. Instead of the toned powerhouse I expected, I saw a faded, melted version of my former face: eye bags, jowls, and wrinkles, like ripples on the edge of the beach where the tide pulls hard. For the next year or two, I experienced the same nanosecond startle when I couldn't avoid the gaze from the glass.

Then I won a "Miracle Makeover" at a raffle. My beauty caboodle included cleanser for my skin type (old), a mysterious "serum," moisturizer, eyebrow pencil, eye shadow, blush, and lipstick. Having once had a department store makeover at the behest of my teen daughter and having watched her *take photos* of the metamorphosis (yes, eyeliner does enhance Nordic eyes), I knew that a dab of makeup *might* make me look as perky as I felt. To give my eager makeover donor honest feedback about her products, I had to use the stuff, and though it might not qualify as a genuine miracle, a subtle change evolved – from the outside, in.

First, I began to wash my face gently every night, not just swipe at it with a washrag. After cleansing, I dabbed on the *solution nocturne*, night lotion, so romantic in French. In the morning, I cleansed again, then petted myself with *solution diurne*, daytime lotion, before the moisturizer. A month into my regimen I wondered, was it my imagination, or did my skin glow, just a teeny-weeny bit? At least it was clean and soft.

In for a penny, in for a pound, I tackled my pale Nordic eyes. I stroked ivory highlighter under my brows feathered with pencil, then a pale shadow and silver blue liner, mascara, add a pouf of blush and lipstick, and I no longer startle when ambushed by mirrors.

173

Do I really appear that much different? No. I've simply become more important to myself. Those eye bags, jowls, and wrinkles haven't gone anywhere. I just like them better. So much better, in fact, that the summer I turned 60, I paid a Québec City street artist to sketch my portrait. Before I sat, I asked Chantal, who was about my vintage, "Do you sketch what you see or the spirit of the person?"

"If I draw you well," she replied, "your spirit will come through." As she sketched, she talked companionably about the difficulty in drawing youngsters like her previous subject, a 9-year-old. "They don't have much contour, much character."

Within a half-hour, she made a final flourish and showed me myself. I gasped. *My goodness! It's me, and I'm beautiful.* "Do I really look like this?" I marveled.

Chantal chuckled, reflecting my pleasure. "*Mais, oui!* But in 20 minutes, I can't put in all the wrinkles. There isn't time!"

My mother loved the portrait when I gave it to her for her 90th birthday. She did not trouble in the least about wrinkles because she was delighted just to be alive, albeit in skin three sizes too big. So is that amazing woman I saw my first day in Collioure.

I walked along the silvery teal sea in the Bay of Collioure where the woodcarver was busily installed working on a low stonewall at the base of the Château. A few paces further along, a woman in a pastel floral tank suit lay on a towel she had draped over the wall, propped on an elbow, her head in her hand. She wore a straw hat at a jaunty angle, huge sunglasses, and a smile. What surprised me, however, was her skin – brown as bourbon and wrinkled as a raisin. She was 80 if she was a day, yet stretched out in confidence to catch the sunshine and, I suspect, admiring glances of what she might once have been – a knockout. She still rejoiced in her body enough to display it. Perhaps she lounged on the low stonewall because she couldn't negotiate the stairs to the adjacent topless beach. Perhaps she was trying to attract a lover or recreate a heady time of lovers long gone by. I tried not to stare, but couldn't help grinning at a feminine ego at its finest, one who blew raspberries to both wrinkles and the Grim Reaper.

Is this elderly woman just affecting a pose on the sunny stonewall? Are her notions of glamour at 80 induced by Alzheimer's or some unusual dementia? I think not. Rather, I think she's utterly honest with herself and those around her. And utterly confident.

And I begin to look at my own body in a more approving way. True beauty, it seems, is less about how we see our appearance and more about how we feel about it. A modest amount of self-confidence is the best cosmetic: no money can purchase it. Without it, all else – clothing, natural beauty (fresh or faded), education – become mere decoration. French women seem to have this confidence in abundance.

The Bay of Collioure bathing beauty stays with me as I learn how to adapt to my maturing femininity. Like her and the Parisian *grande dame* and my dear mother, I must define myself by more than just my body. Sure, when my nurse practitioner sympathized years ago that my "baby factory" was out of business, I mourned the loss for a long, long time, for I cherished my babies and my season of motherhood. I realized then that I am, indeed, more than a baby factory, just as I realize now that I am more than my wrinkles.

So, I'm learning to cherish my precious wrinkled face. I'm rediscovering my own resilient spirit. I am learning elder grace. *Oui,* Monsieur Hugo, I am *adorable.* ###

Chapter 26
Dance On – High Kicks Optional

To dance is to be out of yourself.
Larger, more beautiful more powerful.
This is power on earth and it is yours for the taking.
– Agnes De Mille

In a Latin Quarter tourist shop with the usual assortment of berets, Eiffel Tower key rings, and T-shirts, I spy a lone belly dance top encrusted with sequins and faceted crystals, yellow, red, gold. Strings of sparkling cut glass beads, tiny as rice grains, dangle below the bra, ready to scintillate over undulating abs. What fun! The Middle Eastern sales clerk doesn't even blink when I hold it against my chest. And I remember the stir I created when I took up belly dancing at 60.

"Mo-THER! You've got to be kidding!" squealed my daughters.

"Oh, boy ..." sighed my son in Berkeley. Liberal Berkeley.

"Yes, belly dancing. You told me to exercise more and you're right. Wonderful for the circulation and the abs."

OK, maybe belly dancing is an odd pastime for an overweight Boomer of Swedish descent, but I've loved moving to music ever since I stood on Daddy's feet and thumped around the living room with him, "waltzing" to the radio. My formal dance training began when I took ballet lessons at the "Y." *Arabesque. Plié. Jeté.* How I loved saying them, dancing them. Then came the recital and a crushing disappointment: I was too tall to be a rosebud in Sleeping Beauty's garden. Instead, cast as a butterfly in plain black leotard and orange wings, I flapped around the charmed rosebuds in their coveted pink tutus. No tutu for me. Ever.

Before I could go up on *pointe,* my practical parents signed me up for swimming lessons. So much for dancing until I arrived at college and signed up for ballet, modern, and jazz all in one semester. The crippling workouts didn't stop me. One boring summer, I taught myself the cha-cha from a diagram of how-to footprints in *Seventeen* magazine. Gosh, I loved to dance.

As a young bride, I tried head-snapping Flamenco dance, but whenever I practiced arm flourishes in our basement apartment, I whacked my knuckles on the low ceiling. Still, I kept moving, now with my husband as partner for square dance with matching gingham outfits, frothy petticoat, the works. Later we joined a community theater group in Boston. He made sets; I made the chorus line.

At 26, I took my first tap dance lesson, and as my footwork sped up, I found myself reveling in cardio workouts with top hat and cane. When my husband changed partners and whirled away, I was left dancing solo for the first time in 16 years. Tap dance consoled me. I mean, who can be depressed shuffling off to Buffalo or falling off a log? Riffs and Susie Q's saved my sanity. Then a few years ago, I discovered Contra, the exuberant folk dancing to live fiddle and accordion. This social dancing favors singles. In fact, contra etiquette requires that one dance with everyone else in the hall, so I'm always on the floor at local dances. I've even ventured alone to other cities for festivals where I've stumbled along learning Zydeco, English country, *gavotte*, Israeli, and Balkan styles of dance, a United Nations of movement and joy.

Which brings me back to belly dancing – a joy. I consider the sparkling garment in my hand and mentally address my beloved children far away: *Be glad that your mother is healthy enough to dance and sane enough to recognize that dancing contributes to that health. Be glad that your mother has made peace with the saggy body that gave you life and that continues to serve her well. Be glad that you hear eerie clarinet music and tinkling finger cymbals behind her bedroom door, not the silence of apathetic aging. Yes, your Mom is indulging in a lifelong healthy pleasure. She may be a grandma now, but she's still got to dance.*

I replace the fiery spangled top on the rack, hesitate, then take if off again. No. My mind is made up. I won't buy it. Not my colors. I look better in blues.

This, my final evening in Paris, the sun still shines brightly at 7 p.m., and invites yet more exploration. I board the #69 bus to Champ de Mars and soon arrive at the filigreed underbelly of the Eiffel Tower. Tourists queue to ascend it. Vendors hawk cotton candy, ice cream, and the inevitable tower trinkets. Drawn by "Stayin' Alive" throbbing from a boom box, I weave my way into a small crowd and recognize the young dancers as the Asian and African kids I had seen rehearsing at the Pompidou Center a few weeks ago. Now the African dancer knows the choreography and perfectly mirrors his partner's angular, jabbing moves à la John Travolta. Seeing these two ambitious youngsters once again gives me a pleasant sense of continuity and belonging in this city where I am otherwise anonymous. I want to dance, too, but restrain myself from hogging the limelight and just nod along to the music with the rest of the bystanders. When the music stops, I toss a euro into the hat, wish them well, and continue my walk.

I stroll the Right Bank of the Seine in gathering twilight and once again cross Pont des Arts where thousands of lovers' padlocks twinkle in the last light. *Eh bien*, Mon Cher and I are not destined to have one. My fantasy blew away, and I am scrubbed clean, refreshed, and ready for new experience, a new dance. Hasn't Contra already taught me that not all dances require partners?

For several years now, I've attended folk dance festivals all over New England, usually alone. I love the haunting Balkan music that draws chains of dancers to snake around the room, gathering dancers along the way. Anyone can join these welcoming and inclusive celebrations. Offer your hands. Hold on. Stand behind a competent dancer. Watch her feet. Match her movements. Or for word-bound me, chant directions to myself: *step-right, step-right, back, over-over, pause …* How much easier just to smile and *feel* the rhythm. The pattern will come. Even if my feet make mistakes at first, I can sway my head and shoulders in time with the other dancers and be part of the human kaleidoscope. For the essence of dancing is not perfect technique as much as entering the music, being one with the rhythm and kindred souls. Folk dance, at least, is more about flowing than following.

When I tap danced in my early 30s, I loved the recitals with a half-dozen other mothers known as the Happy Hoofers. We strutted in fishnet hose and spangled costumes on stages no more elaborate than the school auditorium or the VFW Hall. Often the adrenalin rush of performing made me forget subtleties like being on the right foot or turning in the choreographed direction. Marge, my hilarious dance instructor, always laughed at my "free-style" performance. "You're having such a good time and smiling so much, the audience thinks the other dancers are wrong!"

So, too, here in the Paris home of the uninhibited, red-stockinged dancer at the Moulin Rouge of Tom's bon voyage card, I learn the new dances of my 60s, which will sweep me into my 70s and beyond, missteps, be damned. Move. Feel the joy of the music. And sometimes, sometimes, let go of hands, the better to clap my own, and swish my skirt. ###

Chapter 27
Unfinished Woman of a Certain Age

I am not young, but I feel young.
The day I feel old, I will go to bed and stay there.
J'aime la vie! *I feel that to live is a wonderful thing.*
– Coco Chanel

"What do you have to declare?" asks the uniformed customs agent in Boston. I duly describe a few berets, textiles (I don't say "lace bras from Amboise"), a couple of books, and some small artwork: value about $150. He waves me through with a half-smile. "Welcome home."

How simple to explain material things, yet what do I really have to declare from this adventure? What have I brought home with me that has no resale value, that's immune to x-ray, but that has changed me forever?

I left my country as a slightly overweight, uncertain woman *d'un certain âge*, anxious to redeem her self-confidence, afraid of old age, and in love. I've returned 12 pounds lighter, tanned, with arms like Popeye's from hauling my own baggage. My journey through France has reassured me that I can open and close doors, both real and metaphorical. I can solve problems and trust strangers. I can adapt when plans go haywire and even carry on when wounded by a fickle sweetheart.

Most compelling, I've learned that feminine aging can be a beautiful process, and – *quelle surprise*! – growing older does not have to mean becoming ugly or irrelevant. Sure, it was nice to be admired by a man in my life, but after the adrenaline froth of romance subsides, I find that I do not need a romantic fantasy to have a fulfilling life. I've discovered that beauty is an attitude and happiness, a decision. And unless I impose one, there is no statute of limitations on *joie de vivre*.

While waiting to see my obstetrician for a pre-natal check-up more than 30 years ago, I spotted a cartoon in the waiting room. It showed a grinning, white-haired granny crouched on her skateboard zooming up a half-pipe, arms outstretched. The caption read, "Another example of Post-Menopausal Zest." Back then, I thought it was funny. Now, I understand. Parisian Simone would shrug, "*C'est normale. No big deal.*"

About a year after my return, I clean out my freezer as I prepare to move out of my apartment. I find a freezer-burned brook trout Mon Cher caught and left while I was in France. How he valued his catch! Even when we were apart, he sent photos of the big ones.

I remember how he would cook the trout and carefully remove the bones in one fluid movement. So like my life: Extract the prickly bones, expect the occasional jab of a missed one, savor all that's left. The dear man cooked a lot of fish for me in this kitchen. In fact, he insisted upon preparing entire meals while we listened to slow jazz. We drank Chardonnay by candlelight at this table that's now staying behind and watched French movies snuggled on the sofa that I've given to my daughter. All gone ... Interesting guy, Mon Cher. Shall I save that envelope of bougainvillea petals from his Caribbean island?

No time to waste. My well-travelled friend Cynnie, who eagerly supports my writing, travels, and schemes involving both, spends three days helping me to box my dishes, linens, books. Furniture went yesterday. My few possessions, except some clothes and my laptop, are headed for storage in my daughter's basement. Geraniums have gone to Paradise – the library's south window. For the next year or so, I'll alternate house sitting and brief stays with my children and mother to save for my next shoestring excursion. Yes, I'll miss Kitty who will move in with cat-lover friend, Lois, but I can no longer justify working at a job where I'm not appreciated to support an apartment I simply don't need. My son-in-law is allergic to the cat and cannot visit comfortably for more than a few minutes; besides, he and my daughter host holiday gatherings now, not me. And just when I thought the babysitting would never end, it did. My granddaughter stays home alone these days. I'm still important in the lives of my children, but I'm needed now as a trusted consultant, no longer as family CEO.

Now it's my turn.

To squelch serious writing for even one more year has become unthinkable. Already my friends are dying. My high school co-editor Steve died two years ago. Joyce had a stroke last month. If not now, when?

Hurry.

Before Christmas, I begin learning Turkish. Already I can say "hello," "thank you," and "where's the toilet." I book my flights: Paris. Rome. Istanbul. I'll be gone three months. Mon Cher asked to visit before I depart, but now I know better. What he calls love, the kind without heavy lifting, is just erratic companionship such as children enjoy at the playground. No thank you, Mon Cher. I need more. Until I can find it, the world awaits me.

When I was young, I thought grandmothers played out their quiet lives knitting in rocking chairs. Well, I'm off my rocker now – it's in Trina's basement. I toss a handful of coat hangers, a box of Miracle-Gro™, half a head of Romaine, duct tape, and *Guide to Istanbul* on top of the last carton I've wedged into the car. I'm out of bags. *Pas de problème*. I check the rearview, smile at the crow's feet around my I-can't-believe-I'm-doing-this eyes, flip my red scarf over my shoulder, then shift into gear, and confidently glide down the driveway. ###

Acknowledgements

This book would still be just a pleasant reverie if my friends and family hadn't been so bossy.

"Pick a date," said Tom.

"So, go already," said Judy.

"Write it," said Carol, who gave me a ream of paper that Christmas.

Thank you to family and friends who encouraged my Paris dream and nurtured my vision: Tom and Canay Özden Schilling, Trina and Steve Arling, Tess Schilling Fonseca, Greg Schilling, Hannah Schilling, Mindy Carlisle, Marcia Hooper, Deb Lovell, Andy and Angela Parrett, Lois Richard, and Cheryl Williams. You believed in me more than I believed in myself.

Thanks to the library staff at NHTI, Concord's Community College, for throwing my bon voyage party before I decided I'd actually go: Steve Ambra, Joan Malfait, Charlotte Green, Carol Nelson, Joyce Verdone, and Claudette Welch. That red scarf gave me confidence like Dumbo's feather.

Mille mercis to Paula DelBonis-Platt, French table coordinator at NHTI, who helped me to revive French language skills. Also, *mille mercis* to Susan Keane and Liz-

Anne Platt, French editors of the manuscript. You knew what I meant and helped me to write it.

I am grateful for the generous support of the Jentel Artist Community for a month-long residency in Wyoming. Thanks to fellow writers at the New Hampshire Writers' Project and GrubStreet Boston for informative workshops and networking. You helped me to shape my project.

Thanks to those who granted me permission to include quotations: Stacy Allison; and Jonathan Prude, for Agnes De Mille.

I am especially grateful to the early readers who offered insightful critique: Marilú Duncan, Cynnie Irwin, Laura Knoy, Carol Tuveson, and my memoir cohort at the Learning Institute of New England College (LINEC): Sandy Dallaire, Judy Eliasberg, Heleen Kirk, John McCausland, Sue Moore, Claudia Rein, and Abbyann Wasilew. You inspired me to rescue my manuscript and share my story.

Thanks to staff and memoir students at GoodLife Programs and Activities who supported my memoir classes and workshops. Your heartening feedback kept me moving forward.

I am forever indebted to those who offered invaluable editorial guidance: Peg Aldrich, Cynnie Irwin, and Lois Richard. And a huge thank you to Steve Arling for his patient technical support. You are my IT guru.

I can never adequately thank those who offered me a home during the years I gave up my apartment to follow my muse and produce my manuscript: Steve and Trina Arling, Cathy Eaton and Michael Murphy, Becky Field, Tess

Schilling Fonseca, Tareah and Kevin Gray, Greg and Ruth Heath, Joyce Heck, Bunny and Darrell Huddleston, Cynnie and Terry Irwin, Judy and Doug King, Diana and Dan Levine, Joanna and Mark Novembrino, Ercan and Aytül Özden, Brian Pontius, Joan Pontius, Lois and Tom Richard, Stephen Tapscott, Marion Thorell, and Carol Tuveson. You never questioned my nomadic lifestyle and nurtured me when I needed it most.

And one more hug and kiss for my son Tom who sent Mumsy to Paris. ###

Author Information

Gail Thorell Schilling, feature writer, columnist, and teacher, began writing for Rocky Mountain newspapers in 1988 and earned several awards from the Wyoming Press Association. She has contributed to *Daily Guideposts* for more than 20 years. Her freelance writing has appeared in the *Boston Sunday Globe* and regional New Hampshire magazines. Gail has taught writing at colleges in Wyoming and New Hampshire and helped refugees to write their stories. She was awarded a fellowship by the Jentel Artist Community and continues to mentor memoirists of a certain age. Gail lives in Concord, NH. ###

Made in the USA
Middletown, DE
05 September 2019